Shades of Green

by

Julie A. Vincent
&
Robert E. Dittmer

An entertaining and practical guide
to going green your own way
-- at home, at work, and when you travel.

Shades of Green
A guide to going green for the rest of us

iUniverse books may be ordered through booksellers or by contacting:

iUniverse
1663 Liberty Drive
Bloomington, IN 47403
www.iuniverse.com
1-800-Authors (1-800-288-4677)

ISBN: 978-1-4401-7845-0 (pbk)
ISBN: 978-1-4401-7844-3 (ebk)

Printed in the United States of America

iUniverse rev. date: 10/16/2009

Shades of Green

Contents

Shades of Green

Preface

These days, we hear a great deal about how to change the world with our behavior. But it's important to remember that each one of us is a different shade of green.

Most of us recycle waste in some form or another. Some of us harness the energy of solar or wind power in our homes or workplaces. Some eschew SUVs in favor of small, gas-efficient cars, more and more are buying hybrid vehicles and still others ride a bike to work instead of driving. These choices are all dependent upon many factors, such as where we live, how big our family is, how our homes are constructed and what we consume.

This book is about doing what you can – whoever you are and wherever you are – to make our planet healthier by protecting our precious natural resources. *Shades of Green – Going Green Your Way* will provide you with tips and ideas you can use, no matter where you live or what type of lifestyle you lead.

Since you have chosen to pick up this book, you know that no one person can do it all – but we can all make choices that affect the outcomes, in our family, our community, our region, our country, the continent and even the entire world.

Enjoy this book. We hope you have fun with it and share it with others. You may even want to challenge yourself and your family to try to get a little greener each week.

We appreciate all that you are doing to help us save our only home, whatever your shade of green.

Bob McElwee
Publisher: Modern Traveler magazine
Owner: Green Mill Village

Introduction

How to Use This Book

"To be green or not to be green?"

The good news is, this just isn't the question anymore. Of course we must all be green. But how green? Some folks have adopted green practices; others have tried a few lifestyle changes. Most of us want to do our part, but we're not sure where to start. It's OK that we're all approaching "green" from different perspectives. We just have to keep doin' more of what we're doin'. Green is no longer about one person doing a whole lot of "green" things. It's about all of us doing a few more "green" things.

This is the spirit behind this book, *Shades of Green*. It allows readers to start wherever they feel comfortable and in whatever part of the house they'd like. No guilt, no pressure—just a common-sense approach to collectively doing what we can for the environment for ourselves and for our families.

Here's how it works: *Shades of Green* is divided into 12 chapters, ten of which represent a different part of the home. For example, Chapter One discusses things readers can do to adopt more green practices in the kitchen. Chapter Four is about how to make your laundry greener, in terms of both the products we choose as well as the energy we use. Chapter Eight is loaded with hints about recycling, from easy to more advanced. And, there is a chapter on green travel and another on how to be green at the office.

Now here's the fun part. Each chapter is divided into specific problems that are fairly universal and quite solvable. Here's one from the chapter about energy:

> **PROBLEM**: I want to use less energy for heating and cooling my home, not only because it's the right thing to do, but also because energy costs are continually rising. What are some things I can do with my existing equipment or some simple life-style changes I can make now?

Immediately following each problem are realistic, proven tips to solving it. Where this book differs, is that the tips for each problem are arranged by degree of difficulty—three degrees of difficulty, to be exact, from easy to moderate to fairly involved. They are titled as such:

I can do that!

Takin' it to the next level

Dedicated to a green lifestyle

As you begin to read the green tips, get a sense of where you fall. If many of the tips in the "I can do that!" level are things you haven't tried, then that's where you should consider starting. If, after you incorporate most or all of those practices, you feel that's as far as you want to go right now, fine. It all helps. However, if you effortlessly incorporated these practices and have a hunger to do more, proceed to "Takin' it to the next level." If that level encourages you to see the world differently and there's just no going back now, proceed to "Dedicated to a green lifestyle."

Shades of Green

One disclaimer—because the book can be approached from so many different directions and probably not everyone will read every part of the book, you may find some repetition. It was deliberate. So bear with us if you are one of those folks who ends up reading everything. There were just too many great tips that we didn't want readers to miss.

With all this explanation behind us, now it's time to tackle the book—any way you'd like. Pick an area of the house and then a level and get going. Or, decide you want to do the "I can do that!" level for every area of the house and go right through the book in the order it's presented. There's no right or wrong way to approach the book. And, there's no right or wrong way to approach being green—just pick a shade.

Regards,

Julie A. Vincent and Robert E. Dittmer

Chapter One
In the Kitchen

The kitchen—the heart of a home. It's the origin of good food, great family conversation and warm memories we take with us throughout our lives. It's also the room with the biggest potential for waste, both in terms of energy consumption from major kitchen appliances as well as poor food selection and handling.

Did you know kitchen lighting, refrigeration and cooking can be responsible for up to 40 percent of a home's energy consumption, according to U.S. Department of Energy? The good news is that you can cut that percentage by doing some simple things as well as making sound purchases when you're ready to replace major kitchen appliances. And, if you're thinking about a total remodel of your kitchen, you can create a truly green kitchen that will show you and the planet immediate payback.

PROBLEM: We need our kitchen appliances—well, at least most of them—but we're not maximizing the energy. I can't replace my appliances right now, so in the meantime what can I do to save energy?

I can do that!

- Run your dishwasher only when it's full.

Shades of Green

• Skip pre-rinsing lightly soiled dishes before putting them in the dishwasher. You could save about 20 gallons of water per load. If you must pre-rinse, use cold water instead of hot and turn off the faucet while you scrub.

• Keep your microwave clean and it will operate more efficiently.

• Use your microwave as often as possible. It costs about 10 cents to cook one item in your microwave, compared to about 48 cents in a conventional oven. Microwaves are between three and five times more efficient than your oven.

• Foods with a larger surface area cook faster in a microwave. So, for example, when cooking potatoes, cut thin slices as opposed to cubes or quartered pieces. The same goes for heating and steaming vegetables on a regular stove.

• Thaw foods before cooking. Cooking frozen foods uses more energy.

• Aluminum pots and pans are relatively inexpensive and conduct heat quickly. But stainless steel is still the best choice, mainly because it retains heat longer. Ceramics and cast iron also hold heat well.

• Try a pressure cooker, which can save up to two-thirds of the cooking energy. Pressure cookers tend to be a bit expensive to buy, but they last a long time.

• Skip pre-heating your oven if what you're cooking will be in there for an hour or more. There's just no need to heat up the oven with nothing in it. That heats up your kitchen, too.

Shades of Green

• When you're using the oven, try to cook more than one thing at a time.

• Use the right-sized pot for the right-sized burner. About 5 percent of the energy we use is for cooking, so make the most of it.

• Use a lid whenever possible to cut down cooking times.

• Keep your head out of the fridge and keep that door shut. Decide what you want before you open the door.

• Your fridge uses more energy than any of your other kitchen appliances and, in some homes, is the biggest power consumer. So keep the temperature between 38-42 degrees F and your freezer between 0-5 degrees F.

• Fridges are best kept not quite full, so air can circulate properly around the items. Freezers, however, are best kept full.

Takin' it to the next level

• Use cold water when running your disposal.

• When boiling water, boil just the amount you need for the job. You'll save energy as well as conserve water.

• Install a faucet aerator. For a small cost, it's probably the most effective water conservation measure you can put in your kitchen.

• Regularly clean the condenser coils on the back or bottom of your refrigerator. It runs more efficiently.

• Make sure there is enough space between the refrigerator coils and the wall to allow air to circulate efficiently. Trapped heat increases energy consumption.

Dedicated to a green lifestyle

• Contact your local utility to find out what green energy options are available to you.

• Abandon your dishwasher and wash your dishes by hand. If you can't do that, at least stop the machine after the rinse stage and open the door to let dishes air dry.

• Abandon your disposal. Compost your food scraps. You'll have fewer drain problems, have great material for your garden beds and save money on maintaining your septic system.

PROBLEM: The kitchen presents a major opportunity for homeowners to decrease energy consumption. If you have decided to make a major investment in a kitchen remodeling project, how can you be sure you are doing everything you can to go green?

I can do that!

• Purchase only energy-efficient kitchen appliances. Keep in mind that the price tag in the store tells only half the story. It's also what the appliance will cost you to operate over its lifetime. Look for Energy Star-qualified appliances that use advanced technology. These result in 10- to 50-percent less energy and water usage than standard appliances.

Shades of Green

• Although it appears counter-intuitive, energy consumption by the most efficient refrigerator is largely unrelated to its size. Efficient refrigerators are more expensive to buy, but they are high quality and should last longer and need less repair.

• Gas cooking appliances are generally cheaper to operate than electric cooking appliances.

• Think about where you are going to place your refrigerator—don't put it near a heater or in direct sunlight.

• Maximize any available natural light, adding a skylight, if possible. Also consider task lighting, built-in photosensors and programmable controls, which can pay for themselves in a year or less.

• Consider replacing your single-pane windows with Energy Star-qualified windows. These windows use low-e glass with solar shading. You'll have more comfort, less condensation and protection from sun damage, not to mention significant energy savings.

Takin' it to the next level

• With a major remodeling project, you may have the opportunity to add more insulation to your exterior walls. Blowing fibrous insulation material into existing homes will help eliminate moisture problems and air leakage. You can choose from fiberglass material or natural materials such as cellulose and mineral wool.
• If you're going to replace your cabinets, there are many green options. Some cabinets are made from agricultural fiber panels such as wheatboard and strawboard and can be a good choice if moisture is not an issue.

Shades of Green

• If you're going to keep your existing cabinets, there are methods you can use to resurface or reface them, where you can seal older materials that might contain urea formaldehyde. Use low-VOC (volatile organic compounds) paint or stain to seal the old cabinets.

• Always choose low- or no-VOC paints and stains. Most paints and stains contain high levels of VOCs that can produce harmful gasses when applied.

Dedicated to a green lifestyle

• Build in a kitchen recycling center. They are available pre-assembled or as cabinet retrofit kits.

• If you're replacing the kitchen flooring, choose products manufactured from rapidly renewing forests. Environmentally responsible choices include bamboo, cork or eucalyptus. These crops grow to market size in about half the time of hardwoods.

• Choose an induction cook top. Induction cooking generates a magnetic field that induces heat in steel cookware, causing molecules in the pan to move around at high frequencies creating friction or instant heat. These cook tops are the fastest of all types to heat and cook food, and are tremendously more efficient. Their continuous surface is easy to clean and the surface does not heat up. This technology has been around for decades on the commercial restaurant level, but now is available for homes. Your kitchen, however, must be wired for 220 volts and you must use pots and pans made of steel, cast iron or some combination of metals that will react with the magnetic field. The downside? Induction cook tops are expensive.

Shades of Green

- What's even better than an induction cook top? A sun oven! Of course, it must be used outside. But these solar-powered appliances require no fuel and you can use them just like a conventional oven.

Chapter Two:
Foods

Τ*he foods we choose to buy, prepare and eat are critical to our health. Yet there are many foods that will surprise you with their impact on our environment. With to-day's hectic schedules, many of us seek convenience and time-savings, to the detriment of the environment and, maybe, to ourselves and our families.*

With a little education and planning, we can maintain and even improve on a healthy lifestyle, by buying, growing and using more local natural and organic foods. Where foods orig-inate matters. How foods are grown matters. And how food is shipped and packaged matters.

PROBLEM: Most of the food we eat is either trucked or flown from places far, far away, adding to the cost, to greenhouse gases and to the risk of contaminants.

I can do that!

• Check to see where your favorite foods come from. Make every attempt to buy locally. Track your "food miles" and then reduce them. A typical meal, when counting all the ingredients, could have traveled up to 20,000 miles! Long-hauled foods lose nutrients and use fuel to transport. And, the farther away the food comes from and the less you know about the grower, the less you know about possible contaminants.

• Purchase fresh fish instead of canned fish. It saves the energy expended during the canning process and is oftentimes less expensive.

• Replace canned or jarred fruit with fresh fruit. If every U.S. household bought one pound of fresh fruit each month during the summer instead of canned or jarred fruit, the total energy saved could operate kitchen appliances in about 20,000 homes for a year.

• Buy fresh breads from your local bakery. Fresh breads taste great, are packaged in recyclable paper and haven't been frozen or shipped long distances.

• Patronize green restaurants. They use less energy, buy local and organic products and generally incorporate sustainable business practices.

Takin' it to the next level

• Plant your own garden. Reconnect with the earth. And remember, nothing tastes better than your own homegrown tomato!

• Befriend your local farmer. This puts food on your table for the least carbon cost while giving your area farmers a chance of survival. Investigate farmer co-ops in your area and become a steady customer.

• Also befriend your small local grocers, farmers' markets and health food stores.

• Buy organic. Did you know 100,000 organic farms will eliminate almost 12 million cars' worth of CO_2 a year?
• Since the definition of "organic" can vary, make sure your organic purchase was truly grown, raised or pro-

cessed without the use of drugs, synthetic hormones or chemicals, using methods that conserve natural resources and limit the effects on the environment.

• When buying organic, look for the USDA seal. But beware. Some organic products are 100-percent organic; others might be 80-percent or more (or less) organic. And yet others might be "made with organic ingredients."

• Don't confuse organic foods with whole foods or natural foods. While they are all similar, the requirements for organic foods are much more defined than for natural and whole foods. Generally, natural foods do not include synthetic ingredients; whole foods tend to maintain their nutrients because they are processed as little as possible.

Dedicated to a green lifestyle

• If you decide to live off your land, make sure you use natural means of weed and bug control instead of pesticides and other harmful chemicals. Seek the advice of local growers and gardeners who know what problems you might encounter and how to best solve them naturally.

• Use natural fertilizers like grass clippings and leaves to enrich the soil. Add mulch and compost to help retain water.

• Buy organic seeds that are USDA-certified. They will not have any genetic modifications.

• Make sure some plants in your garden also don't serve another, less desirable, function. For example, herbs like cilantro and dill are great to add to your cooking, but also attract natural predatory insects such as ladybugs.

• Buy sustainably harvested wild fish, as opposed to farmed varieties. Farmed fish tend to have higher heavy metal levels and, because the fish live in extremely close quarters, they generate concentrated amounts of feces.

• Eat lower on the food chain. It takes less energy for fruit and vegetable production than for meat production.

• Cut off all excess fat from meat and poultry and avoid high-fat dairy products. Fat can be a collector of chemicals in the environment.

• Replace meat with soy products. Soy products are better for you, and growing soybeans doesn't take as much water as livestock production.

PROBLEM: It's not just our food we need to think about. We should also make better drinking choices, too. The average American drinks about two liters of some form of liquid each day. Consider bottled water, for example. It may be commercially successful, but the environment is paying a heavy price.

I can do that!

• Abandon buying individual bottled water and drink the water from your tap instead. Studies show that tap water is actually held to more stringent quality standards than some bottled water, and some brands are even just tap water in disguise. About 1.5 million barrels of oil are used to make the individual plastic water bottles each year, not to mention the thousands of gallons of oil it takes to transport them to stores. In addition, only 10 percent of water bottles are recycled, leaving the rest in landfills where it takes thousands of years for the plastic to decompose. That's a lot of bottles, considering the average American consumes 166 bottles of water each year.

• Limit your purchase of individual bottled water for when you're traveling in countries where water quality is questionable.

• If you don't like the taste of your tap water, buy an inexpensive water filter pitcher or install an inexpensive faucet filter to remove trace chemicals and bacteria.

• When traveling, or even when shopping and running errands, fill a reusable water bottle from your tap and take it with you. After you're through with it for the day, make sure to wash it with hot, soapy water, giving special attention to the neck of the bottle, then let it air dry. And make sure your water bottle is just yours. Family members should have their own water bottles.

• The next time you buy drinks, choose those in glass bottles instead of aluminum cans. The energy it takes to make a 12-ounce aluminum can is enough to produce two new 12-ounce bottles. And, of course, recycle the glass bottles when you're through with them.

Takin' it to the next level

• Purchase teas that have been environmentally grown. Organizations such as the USDA and the Organic Trade Association encourage environmentally friendly methods of growing tea that avoid the use of pesticides, herbicides and synthetic fertilizers.

• Orange juice can be green, too. Choose organic orange and other fruit juices.

• There are many organic wines, too. Simply look for the certified organic designation. For a wine to be labeled "100-percent organic," the grapes must have been grown in completely organic conditions with no sulfites added.

• Look for organic beer or buy your beer from a nearby winery or micro brewery. Your purchase will reduce fossil fuel consumption because you're buying locally. You'll also help your local community.

• Look for organic spirits. Although harder to come by, there are organic spirits on the market such as vodka, gin, rum and tequila.

Dedicated to a green lifestyle

• Abandon soda. Soda consumption has skyrocketed, making up about 28 percent of all drinks consumed. Search for drink choices made from organic fruit juices, seltzer water (which is filtered water that has been carbonated), teas and other great options. You'll lose 17 teaspoons of sugar and about 250 calories per drink by switching.

• Think about eliminating or decreasing consumption of cow's milk, choosing soy, rice or almond milk options instead. You'll avoid ingesting hormones and antibiotics. Plus, how dairy cows live and how they are fed have fueled controversy in recent years. The use of pasture land, the energy needed on a dairy farm to keep milk production up and cows' contribution to the global emissions of methane (about 28 percent) are all considerations.

• Buy fair-trade, shade grown coffee. Also look for Bird Friendly or Rainforest Alliance certification seals. These labels represent coffee farms that practice sustainable agriculture.

• Learn how to make your own beer and wine. Organic ingredients can be purchased at local farmers' markets or maybe even at your grocery store. Check online for instructions and supplies, too.

PROBLEM: As a country, we waste so much food!

I can do that!

• Take good care of your leftovers and other perishable foods that you buy. Make use of everything and don't forget about these foods until they have spoiled and you have to throw them away. Write dates on the leftover boxes and other food packaging.

• Plan your meals so that items bought and portions sizes fit your needs. Cooking more than you need is fine, as long as you have a plan for those leftovers so nothing is wasted. In fact, making enough food for more than one meal saves energy and probably some money, too.

Takin' it to the next level

• Keep your kitchen scraps from fruits, vegetables and coffee grounds in a composting bin or container. The compost is great for your garden. And organic waste that's diverted from the landfill really adds up.

• Bring your lunch to work. It's a great way to make sure you use leftovers and other perishable food, and you'll save money, too! Make it a habit not to waste anything.

• Be aware of food drives in your area and participate. Don't know of a food drive? Then organize one yourself and give to a worthy and knowledgeable not-for-profit organization.

Dedicated to a green lifestyle

• Ask your favorite restaurants, your company cafeteria and other food establishments what they do with their leftover food at the end of the day. Many cities and towns have not-for-profit groups that reallocate this perfectly good food to those in need.

• Call your area grocers and ask what they do with dented cans and food or drink items that have come unpackaged and can't be sold as is. Many grocers donate these food items that are perfectly fine.

• If your area does not have an organization that distributes leftover food, start one.

PROBLEM: Paper or plastic? How about neither!

I can do that!

• Say no to plastic bags from the grocery. Each one can

take 1,000 years to decompose. Studies show a mere 1 percent actually get recycled. And up to 3 percent of all plastic bags become litter. Plus, plastic bags are made from crude oil and natural-gas derivatives. Some sources say the manufacturing of plastic bags uses 12 million barrels of crude oil each year.

• When eating out, don't grab a handful of paper napkins. One or two will usually do. Think about the waste. You probably don't put 12 napkins on your dinner table, so why do it when you're eating out?

• Stop using or at least decrease your use of paper towels. If you must wean yourself from paper towels, start by buying the rolls that are perforated in a way that allows you size choices. Better yet, though, use cloth rags.

Takin' it to the next level

• Take a step further than just asking for paper bags— bring reusable bags with you. There are many fun reusable, trendy and inexpensive bags from which to choose.

• Abandon the individual one-use water bottles. Take along your own refillable water bottle instead. And how about using a travel mug for coffee instead of getting coffee everyday in a disposable cup?

• Use the paper and plastic bags that do make it home to line your wastebaskets and garbage cans instead of buying plastic trash liners. If you must buy plastic liners, choose a brand with 100-percent post-consumer recycled content.

Shades of Green

Dedicated to a green lifestyle

• Stop using all disposable cups, paper plates, plastic utensils and paper napkins.

• Pack a waste-free lunch for the kids. Eliminate plastic bags, paper napkins, plastic utensils and those brown paper bags and instead choose reusable items.

• Make a real effort to buy products that come in the least amount of packaging, when possible. About $1 of every $11 spent at the grocery goes toward packaging. Consumer pressure can make a difference. Big-box retailers are exerting their power to eliminate oversized and over wrapped packaging for their private-label products. One retailer has already had 500 private-label products packaging redesigned to be less harmful to the environment, eliminating PVC plastic and excess wrapping.

• Try to buy more items in bulk. The items could cost up to 50 percent less and you will reduce the amount of packaging. Buying items in larger-sized cans can also reduce the amount of steel used.

• Don't use plastic bags or plastic storage containers. Use glass or porcelain containers instead. You'll help the environment and stop chemicals from leeching into your food.

Chapter Three:
Cleaning Materials

*I*n *our homes, businesses and hobbies we use chemical cleaning materials all the time. We like our homes clean and sanitary, especially the kitchen and bathrooms. Our dishes, our furniture, our floors, our windows, our clothes, the car--all get close attention. And we use cleaning materials – chemicals in many cases – to accomplish this goal. While business and industry are the most prolific users of these chemicals, the average person uses plenty of chemicals.*

We all grew up with these cleaners. Many of them are petroleum-based and have negative effects on the environment. Even worse, many of these cleaning materials are toxic to our environment! Many man-made chemicals are poison to animals, plants, trees and our water. Many are even poison to US! In fact:

¤ *There are 17,000 petrochemicals available for home use today, but only 30 percent of those have ever been tested for exposure to humans and our environment.*

¤ *There are 63 synthetic chemical products found in the average American home. That's roughly 10 gallons of harmful chemicals.*

¤ *The institutional cleaning industry uses about five billion pounds of chemicals each year.*

These chemicals are not only waste, adding to a growing

problem of waste management, they are also toxic waste. Toxic to the environment and toxic to us. And, if they are petroleum-based, they're made from a diminishing resource.

It's not that we have been criminally polluting the earth for years. Our motivations were pure. Clean and sanitary. But we now know that many of these chemicals are damaging our earth.

So what do we do about that? Can we do anything?

Yes. There are many natural alternatives to the chemicals and cleaning materials we now use. This chapter presents you with many different options.

PROBLEM: Our kitchen and bathroom cleaners, for dishes, for countertops, for tables, for toilets -- for just about everything -- are composed of toxic and petroleum-based chemicals. We need to replace them with more environmentally friendly products.

I can do that!

• OK, here's one that's so simple you will be surprised – and maybe even a little skeptical. You don't need those expensive germ killing antibacterial and antimicrobial cleaners! The FDA has already clearly reported that they don't do any better than plain soap and water. So use just soap and water. The outcome is fewer super-bugs building resistance to our antibacterials. Your kitchen is just as clean, and your products are just as protected against bacteria.

• Stop using those spray cans of air freshener in the kitchen. They contain all sorts of chemicals. Your grandma knew what to do, use baking soda. It does a great job of soaking up the odors. By the way, baking soda in your fridge will also absorb odors and strange smells. And baking soda will remove odors from your carpet. Just sprinkle a little on the carpet and then vacuum it.

• When cleaning kitchen surfaces, consider using vinegar (aka acetic acid). Vinegar is a mild disinfectant and cuts grease, cleans glass quite effectively, deodorizes, and removes calcium deposits, stains and wax build-up. Yes, you have to put up with the smell briefly, but it's much more environmentally friendly.

• Did we mention baking soda? Oh, yeah. A great, mildly abrasive and gentle cleaner just right for countertops. It's a good scrubbing cleaner for stainless steel, iron and copper pots. It's also excellent for chrome or enamel.

• Check those soap containers for their ingredients. Many are full of chemicals. Yet the basis for most cleaning soaps is – well, pure soap. Pure soap, without synthetic scents, colors and other additives, will clean just as effectively as the commercial brands. It biodegrades safely and completely and is non-toxic to humans or the environment.

• When you toss those cleaning products, don't just throw them in the trash or down the sink. If they are toxic in your house, they'll be toxic in the landfill or the water supply. Save them for those community recycling days dedicated to chemicals, oils and lubricants. They'll end up being handled correctly.

• Here's a simple one: when you buy your cleaning materials, buy in concentrated form. Why? You're saving on packaging, which is almost always plastic (which is non-biodegradable).

Shades of Green

Takin' it to the next level

• Stop with the disposables already! Disposable paper towels, disposable wipes and disposable and artificial sponges all have chemicals in them and end up in land-fills and water tables. Instead, use cloth and microfiber wipes. You can clean them with soap and water in the dishwasher. If they need whitening, use hydrogen per-oxide – also a natural product.

• If you want to use sponges, buy natural sponges, not artificial. Just make certain they come from a commer-cial sponge farm and not the natural environment.

Dedicated to a green lifestyle

• Create your own cleaning materials. You can make them from products you have around the house. It will save you money and be friendlier to the environment. Here are four quick ideas for mixing your own cleaners:

¤ Baking soda cleaner: mix a quarter-cup of baking soda with one quart of warm water to make a good cleaning solution.

¤ Mix two parts borax with one part lemon juice and olive oil for polishing unvarnished furniture. Just be careful with borax. Limit its use to this one.

¤ For varnished furniture, use half a cup of warm water and a few drops of lemon juice.

¤ Clean your windows with a solution of a quar-ter-cup of rubbing alcohol mixed with half a cup of vinegar and two cups of water. Instead of paper towels, use newspaper to wipe the windows.

¤ Note: Some will suggest ammonia as a cleaner. While ammonia is very effective at cleaning, deodorizing and disinfecting, it is also very harsh. It can irritate the eyes, nose, throat and skin and can cause headaches, nausea and chest pains. For these reasons, we suggest you not consider ammonia as a cleaning agent.

PROBLEM: Our other household cleaners also need to be addressed and modified or reduced. We need to replace them with more environmentally friendly products.

I can do that!

• Don't wash the car in the driveway. When you do, you wash soap and other harmful chemicals into the sewer system. This strains the system, pollutes the water table, and introduces harmful chemicals into the ecosystem. Instead, use commercial car washes. They usually have to have a permit from their local municipality to operate and that usually means requirements to properly handle detergents and solvents used in the process. Spend those few dollars. It's actually better for the environment.

• We all get our carpets cleaned routinely, at least once a year or more often. When you shop for carpet cleaning firms, look for those that use only water or natural solvents. They'll usually tell you that in their advertising or marketing materials. Make certain it's steam cleaning, not chemical cleaning.

• Believe it or not, cornstarch makes a great tool for removing fat or oil stains. And cornstarch is all natural and fully biodegradable.

• Buy "green cleaners" now coming on the market. But make certain you read the labels. Make sure the cleaner lists all natural products in the ingredients. Avoid anything with petroleum-based solvents, chlorine, glycol ethers or dyes of any kind. Look for language that indicates they are nontoxic and biodegradable. It may take a little looking, but more and more of these cleaners are becoming available. If you don't want to pay the premium many of these products are charging, create your own.

Takin' it to the next level

• Shop your clothes cleaner and laundry. Conventional dry cleaners are among the largest users of industrial solvents. One, Perchloroethylene (called PERC) is toxic to humans and is one of the chemicals that create smog. There are other methods that are much friendlier to the environment. Look for cleaners that use green methods in their processes. Two are called Green Earth (they use a silicone-based solvent which is non-toxic) and liquid carbon dioxide cleaning. If you must continue to use a conventional cleaner, make certain you air out your clothes after delivery to remove chemical traces. By the way, Consumer Reports tested these two methods and compared them to conventional dry cleaning. They found both were more effective in cleaning clothes than dry cleaning!

• Store bought air fresheners are full of chemicals. Try some alternatives. Boil cinnamon, cloves or other herbs. Experiment with various herbs to find what you like. Bake some fresh chocolate cookies and put that wonderful scent in the air.

Shades of Green

• Consider your interior design. Add plants to your rooms to help filter inside air. Almost any broad leaf green plant will do, pick what you like. Plants will not generally make the house smell better, but will help filter the air since they use carbon dioxide and return oxygen to the atmosphere.

Dedicated to a green lifestyle

• To really do it right, consider replacing your carpet with other flooring materials. Consider wood, linoleum, tile, or even laminates. These don't require stringent cleaning materials – natural soap and water usually work just fine with them.

• All home appliances and furniture tend to give off chemicals and gasses (called outgassing). Get rid of anything with PVCs (polyvinyl chloride). The product will be called plain vinyl. Everything about PVCs is bad, from original source, through manufacturing to your home.

Some additional toxic chemical information: the following chemicals are those to watch for. They are all toxic. Read product labels and avoid any products with these chemicals. Many are banned in Europe and other countries.

1. Phthalate family of chemicals. Included in this group are dinbutyl phthalate (DBP) and diphthalate (DEMP). A carcinogen that has been linked to such problems as birth defects, damage to reproductive organs, and lung, liver and kidney cancers. Look for this chemical in nail polish, hair-straighteners, body lotions and deodorants.

Shades of Green

2. Laryl sulfate and sodium laureth sulfate. These chemicals are suspected carcinogens linked to kidney and liver damage, cataract development, eczema and dermatitis. They are often found in toothpaste, shampoo and shower gels.

3. Paraben preservatives (alkyl-p-hydroxybenzoates). The various forms of this chemical have been linked to breast cancer, skin rashes, and hormone disruption. You will find them in conditioners, hair styling gels, nail cream, mascara, skin creams and facial masks. They are also in deodorants, sunscreen and hair coloring.

4. Amin family Diethanolamine (DEA) and others (triethanolamine, and amonoethanolamine). These chemicals can result in hormone disruption, have been linked to cancer of the liver and kidney, and can cause contact dermatitis. Look for them in shampoos and soaps, hairsprays, sunscreens, eyeliners, talc, shaving creams and hair coloring products.

5. Propylene or Butylene Glycol. Has been linked to possible brain, liver and kidney disorders, respiratory problems, pulmonary edema, hypoglycemia and skin rashes. You will find them in deodorants, body lotions, hair gel, hand-wipes and lipsticks.

Chapter Four:
In the Laundry

We love clean clothes, so we regularly wash everything. And rightly so. Isn't cleanliness appropriate? Sanitation important? Sure. But, are we
doing it the right way? Are we conscious of the energy and
water usage the standard laundry room takes? How about all
those detergents. Know what's in them? Are they all environmentally benign?

In 1997 alone, the Poison Control Center reported 230,000
people who received excess exposure to household cleaners
that caused health problems. Seven of them died! Do you
want these same chemicals in your drinking water? They'll
get there when you pour that old cleaner down the toilet or
throw it away.

While cleanliness is next to godliness, perhaps we can be a
little more respectful of our environment by paying more attention to the details of our washing, and perhaps spending a
little more effort as well.

Here are some good ideas to be a more environmentally friendly laundry operator.

Shades of Green

PROBLEM: The average washing machine uses huge amounts of water every wash cycle. Can we control that better?

I can do that!

• Wash only what you really need to wash. Not everything needs to be washed after every use. Underclothing, OK. Outer wear – well, be a discerning judge about when to wash. In the U.S. we tend to wear out our clothes washing them, not wearing them.

• Only wash when you can do a full load. Doing partial loads for convenience only uses extra water since some machines don't allow you to set water levels.

Takin' it to the next level

• Replace those older washing machines with new, high-efficiency models. They will save energy, but they also use less water that older machines, have unique settings for determining loads, and save significant amounts of water. As an example, when compared to washing machines that are only 10 years old, new high efficiency machines use nearly 400 gallons of water less on an annual basis.

Dedicated to a green lifestyle

• Wash as much by hand as you reasonably can. Lots of clothing today will stand up to simple hand washing like our grandparents did, and still look great.

Shades of Green

PROBLEM: The average laundry uses far too much energy. Can we do a better job at that?

I can do that!

• Again, use your washing machine only when you have a full load.

• Clean that lint screen regularly. You'll save as much as 5 percent on your electricity bill.

• Stop using the hot wash cycle. As much as 90 percent of the energy used for washing your clothes is spent on heating the water! Use warm when necessary, cold as often as possible. If you wash in cold water only, you'll save 90 percent of the energy cost of that wash load.

• When you leave home for trips or vacations, unplug your washer and dryer. Why? They all have standby modes that use electricity. Just doing this could save as much as 5 percent on your electricity costs.

Takin' it to the next level

• Your old washing machine is an energy hog! New high-efficiency models use less than .9 kilowatt hours per washing load, significantly less than older machines.

• Look for front-loading washers and dryers. They are much more efficient and wash and dry clothes faster.

• For both your washing machine and your clothes dryer, always buy Energy Star products. These machines meet strict energy usage guidelines set by the U.S. Department of Energy and U.S. Environmental Protection Agency.

• There are new washing machines that are called "hot fill." They connect directly to your water heater. This takes a bit of technology to hook up, so have a plumber with the right expertise do the hookup. It saves heating the water in the washing machine – you already have hot water in an efficient hot water heater.

• Get a washing machine that has a fast final spin cycle. Look for 1,600- or even 1,800- rpm models. This nearly halves the energy you will use for drying because it gets more of the water out of your clothes.

• Another much more energy efficient dryer option is now available--the gas-fired clothes dryer. The gas-fired clothes dryer is a great alternative, especially if you already have gas coming to your house. It uses 60 percent less energy (including the gas costs) and dries 40 percent faster than electric dryers.

Dedicated to a green lifestyle

• Ready? Consider drying your clothing the natural way when weather and climate allow. Yes, air dry outside (or even inside). It's much more environmentally friendly and will save you energy costs and cut down on pollutants in the air. How much pollution? Save up to 700 pounds of CO_2 alone just by air drying your clothes six months out of the year!

Shades of Green

PROBLEM: We use lots of detergents and chemicals to clean our clothes. Many of these are manufactured using toxic chemicals with complex names. Are there alternatives?

I can do that!

• The best cleaner made is still SOAP. Soap will clean just about anything. But, start by getting pure soap without chemical additives like scents and oils. Many of these are created with chemicals.

• Rule of thumb: if there are any warnings on the product label about "avoiding contact," "may cause skin irritation," or "use in a well-ventilated area" that suggests a product you don't want to have in your home.

• For washing your clothes, find a vegetable-based detergent. You can usually find them in health stores.

Takin' it to the next level

• Learn the difference between soap and detergent. Both use surfactants, organic molecules that help get between the grime and fabric. But soaps tend to be organically based, meaning they are derived from plant or nut oils. Detergents are synthetic and are usually made from petrochemicals. Buy soaps and then, if stains persist, try some of the ideas below.

• Before treating a stain, decide if it's organic or protein. Examples of organic and protein stains include blood, sweat or coffee. These are easily removed with hydrogen peroxide. Fatty stains, like those from salad dressings, usually come out by applying cornstarch. Fruit stains usually come out when drenched in boiling water.

• When you must use a detergent, use as little as possible. We all tend to use too much soap and detergent to get the job done. And make sure you notice if a label says "ultra." That means it's concentrated and you can get away with using even less.

Dedicated to a green lifestyle

• Make your own detergents. This is not as hard as it seems. Here are some ideas:

¤ Laundry soap: Add baking soda (aka washing soda) to the wash cycle to boost cleaning and cut back on your regular detergent. Make sure you use a non-phosphate detergent.

¤ Instead of commercial bleach, use hydrogen-peroxide (3 percent). Instead of adding it to the wash, spot clean.

¤ Stop using commercial fabric softeners. Instead, use regular vinegar. Add one to two cups to the rinse cycle of your washer to deodorize and soften your clothes.

¤ For stain removal, use equal parts vinegar and water. Mix the two and use the result to remove tough stains. It works great on grass stains, perspiration, rust, jam, coffee, orange juice, wine, beer, ketchup, barbeque sauce, chili, urine and pet stains.

¤ Lemon juice often works quite well on stains.

Chapter Five:
In the Bathroom

In the bathroom live germs – and we hate germs. Yet we go way overboard killing those guys. And we use far too many chemicals cleaning ourselves in the shower and tub.

Here too we find our cosmetics, hair care, and other personal products. All too often, unfortunately, filled with toxic and dangerous chemicals.

And, of course, here we use two major precious resources: water and energy. We use too much of both. Worse, all those chemicals in our personal hygiene products end up washing down the drain and finding their way into our water supply. Even worse than that, our waste water treatment facilities often cannot handle many of these chemicals. So they end up in our water, our food, our children...and so on. Do we like that idea? No.

Yet, we can't do without any of it. So here we provide you with lots of great ideas on how you can reduce your chemical impact on the environment, save energy, and save water – protecting our natural resources.

PROBLEM: What's with all those cleaning products we use in the bathroom? They all appear to have strong chemicals that seem toxic. Are there alternatives?

Shades of Green

I can do that!

• Start by ensuring that you don't pour stuff down the sink that shouldn't be there! Don't let grease, solvents, oils, or anything like that go down the drain. Save them for the recycle center.

• Install a drain sieve to protect the drain from particulate matter that would otherwise escape into the sewers.

• We often loose hair in the shower. It happens to all of us. Just don't let it wash down the drain. Collect it and set it aside. Throw it away in the trash later (yes, it's fully biodegradable!). Why not let it go into the drain? Because it will serve as a trap for other items – and chemicals – to be caught in your pipes. Eventually it will either clog your drains, or, worse, it will get loose into the sewer with all those chemicals attached.

• Instead of using tub and tile cleaners with chlorine (most have it!), use a stiff bristled brush and baking soda routinely.

Takin' it to the next level

• Read the labels of all cleaners before you buy. If it has any warnings about skin sensitivity, breathing, or special precautions, don't buy it and don't use it. If it has chlorine in the composition, forget it.

• Once a week, clean your drains with a mixture of baking soda and salt. Mix one cup of baking soda with one cup of salt and pour it into the drain. Follow that with a rinse of boiling water and then rinse again with cold water.

• For mold and mildew, try vinegar saturated into a cloth. Then scrub with a stiff brush or an old toothbrush.

Dedicated to a green lifestyle

• Commit to never using a commercial chemical-based cleaner again. Do your research and discover other natural products that will accomplish the cleaning tasks you need done in the bathroom.

PROBLEM: So what about makeup? Do I need to do something different? Yes, makeup is composed mostly of chemicals, most of which have never been tested or certified by independent analysis or the government for their safety. Moreover, none of those companies is concerned with the residue that ends up in our water and landfills.

I can do that!

• Start by educating yourself on what chemicals are in the cosmetics you use today. Visit www.cosmeticdatabase.com. This a website supported by the Environmental Working Group. On the site they maintain a searchable database of cosmetics called Skin Deep. The database will suggest the toxicity of many commercial cosmetic products. Then you be the judge.

• Here are some very simple guidelines:

  ¤ Be sure to read the labels. Watch for warnings to avoid skin contact and ingestion.

Shades of Green

¤   Use mild soaps, not strong ones. They can re-move the skin's natural moisturizers.

¤   Avoid dark hair dyes. They more often than not contain coal tar. Nasty stuff.

¤   Try to cut back on the number and amount of cosmetic products you use.

¤   Lessen your use of colognes and perfumes. Many fragrances have phthalates and parabens. Both are health risks.

• Avoid companies that use animal testing on their products. While progress is being made on reducing animal testing for cosmetics, we are not there yet. Visit www.leapingbunny.org/shopping_guide for guidance on products that don't use animal testing.

Takin' it to the next level

• Go for the natural and organic products. From face cleaners to foundations, there are a lot of new products available today that use natural ingredients safe for you and much better for the environment. As always, how-ever, read the labels.

• Stop with the hair coloring. There's noting wrong with your hair color the way it is. Not all of us need to be blondes, and gray is also a beautiful color. The dyes in hair coloring are full of chemicals – most of them bad for you and bad for the environment.

• OK, we have to talk about it. Feminine hygiene prod-ucts. Once used, these paper products end up in land-fills and create waste, or are incinerated. Consider reusable tampons and sanitary napkins. These products are made from cotton and other natural substances, and can be washed and reused.

Dedicated to a green lifestyle

• Quit chemical cosmetics all together. Even natural and organic products still rob from our environment, put unnatural substances on you skin and body, and cost energy to manufacture. Most of us are born with sufficient inner and outer beauty that we don't need much enhancement.

PROBLEM: We use too much water in the average American bathroom. How can we reduce our water consumption?

Editors Note: We cover water issues extensively in Chapter Nine. Here are just some of those ideas as they pertain specifically to the bathroom.

• Here's a simple one: just turn off the water while you are brushing your teeth! While that toothbrush and toothpaste is doin' its thing, running water accomplishes nothing other than wasting water. Just turn off the water while you brush, then turn it back on to rinse. Water companies suggest the savings from this simple action alone will amount to a saving of seven gallons a minute!

• Do the same while you are shaving. Turn off the water while slicing off that hair, then turn it on again to rinse. Another seven gallons per minute!

Shades of Green

• Check your sink and toilet for leaks. A leaking toilet can use 90,000 gallons of water in just one month. Fix as necessary.

• Check your faucet for drips. A dripping faucet can waste as much as 20 gallons a day! Fix as necessary.

• Take shorter showers. Reducing your time in the shower by just a few minutes can save 20 to 30 gallons of water each day.

• If you like baths fill the tub half-full instead of completely full. You will still get clean and save up to 4,500 gallons of water a year.

• Flush less. During the California drought many operated on the following principle: "When it's brown, flush it down; when it's yellow, let it mellow." They cut their water usage significantly. You can too.

• Don't let the water just run while you wait for hot water. While you are waiting for hot water, brush your teeth or wash your hands and face. Make use of the water. Don't let it just go down the drain.

Takin' it to the next level

• Install a low-flow shower head. This simple action that costs less than $30 can save as much as five gallons of water a minute.

• Install faucet aerators on your faucets. They cost pennies and deliver as strong a flow as without. But, they can reduce your water use as much as 50 percent!

Shades of Green

Dedicated to a green lifestyle

• Install a new, low-flow toilet. These new toilets use only 1.6 gallons per flush instead of 3.5 to 7 gallons for older toilets. You can cut your water usage by as much as 20 percent just with this one action. That means a family of four saves 4,000 gallons of water a year!

• There are now new systems that allow you to use the water from the tank refilling to wash your hands first after using the toilet. That's using the water twice.

PROBLEM: We also use too much energy in the bathroom. The greatest energy user in the bathroom is heating water for showers and baths. What are some ways to reduce energy consumption just in the bathroom?

I can do that!

• Start by taking a shorter shower. Yes, it will save water. But it will also save energy because you don't have to heat more water. Heating anything requires a great deal of energy.

• Stop taking baths, if that is your inclination. Or at least reduce the number. Baths take about twice the hot water as showers.

• Turn the lights off when you are not in the bathroom. Far too many of us leave the lights on constantly. The bathroom is often the best lighted room in the house, of necessity, but correspondingly uses more energy than other rooms. Just making sure the lights are on only when you need them will save you as much as 5 percent of your electricity costs per month.

Shades of Green

Takin' it to the next level

• Replace your current water heater. Look for two things: efficiency and size. Many families start with large 70-gallon water heaters for adults and kids. Later, with the kids gone, they are still heating 70 gallons of water. Downsize.

• Make sure your hot water pipes are wrapped all the way to the faucet. Especially look at pipes with exterior exposures. This often happens in bathrooms with outside walls. In cold climates, you can lose as much as 50 percent of the heat just through transmission.

• Replace all you bathroom light bulbs with CFLs. These are modern fluorescents that are much more efficient and use only one quarter of the electricity of traditional incandescent light bulbs. Major energy savings are possible here.

Dedicated to a green lifestyle

• Install a "flash heater" for hot water in your bathroom. These devices quickly heat just enough water for your bathroom sink. You don't wait for hot water to come to you and you don't need a 70-gallon hot water heater just for your morning routines. While not inexpensive, they will save you money and energy over just a few years.

• Replace your bathroom lights. Many bathrooms actually have too much lighting. And it's often badly designed to provide light everywhere in the bathroom instead of directly in places where light is important – like directly on you at the sink, or in the shower. Take a close look at your lighting plan and redesign it for efficiency.

Chapter Six:
Energy Actions

*A*mericans sure know how to use—and waste—energy. In fact, nearly half of all energy used in our homes is wasted. Heating and cooling inefficiencies are the major cause. But don't despair! There are many inexpensive ways to cut your energy costs without compromising your comfort. And some changes don't cost anything at all. They just take a little thought and a little cleaning up of some bad habits.

PROBLEM: I want to use less energy for heating and cooling my home, not only because it's the right thing to do, but also because energy costs are continually rising. What are some things I can do with my existing equipment or some simple lifestyle changes I can make now?

I can do that!

• What's the simplest way to immediately reduce your heating costs? Put on a sweater!

• Adjust your climate by two degrees. Turning your heat down two degrees in the winter and your air conditioning up two degrees in the summer can save you money. The U.S. Department of Energy reports about

Shades of Green

45 percent of the average utility bill goes to heating and cooling a home. Nationwide, that accounts for the production of about 150 million tons of carbon dioxide.

• Maintain your current heating and air-conditioning equipment by having annual clean-and-check inspections.

• Change or clean furnace filters regularly. Clogged filters reduce air flow and cause the furnace to work harder, using more energy. Severely clogged filters can even lead to compressor damage. To check a filter, hold it up to a light and see if light shines through. The rule of thumb is to change a furnace filter every three months of furnace use.

• Keep the area around your furnace clear of clutter. Nothing should be leaning against it or near your pilot light.

• Keep your ductwork clean.

• Make sure your registers and air returns are unobstructed.

• Make sure your fireplace damper is closed when the fireplace is not in use.

• And, of course, turn off all lights when not in use.

Takin' it to the next level

• Check your ductwork for any leaks.

• Draft proof your home. A simple way to locate drafts is with the use of a stick of incense or a "smoke pencil."

Shades of Green

Simply choose a breezy day, light the incense or smoke pencil and walk around windows, doors, fireplace and areas where plumbing and wiring go through walls. If your smoke drifts horizontally, you have a serious air leak. Most leaks can be quickly plugged with exterior silicone caulk. Be sure to caulk the leaks from the outside of the house or else moisture will build up inside the walls.

• Purchase and install plastic window kits to prevent drafts and fill gaps. The kits contain sheets of plastic film and double-sided tape. Simply cut the plastic to fit your window, place on your window with tape and then heat with a hair dryer to shrink the plastic sheeting tight.

• If your doors are the source of a draft, apply weather-stripping. Or consider door sweeps. Door sweeps are available at most hardware stores and are relatively inexpensive and easy to install. A door sweep cuts down on the "pull" when the heated air inside a home "pulls" on outside colder air, drawing it in.

• Use your drapes and shades to your advantage. Let sunlight in during the day in cold weather and keep cold air away at night. In warm weather, shut the drapes to keep out the excess heat. Lined drapes are best. If your drapes are not lined, consider lining them yourself with something as simple and inexpensive as an old bed sheet.

• Install a programmable thermostat to adjust the times the house is heated or cooled throughout the day and night. You can save as much as 10 percent of your heating costs by turning down your thermostat 10 to 15 percent for eight hours a day, either while you're at work or while you're sleeping.

• Consider adding ceiling fans. They help with both heating and cooling, but make sure you buy units that are reversible. In winter, the blades should rotate clockwise; in summer, counterclockwise. To realize the most energy savings from the addition of ceiling fans, adjust your thermostat accordingly. For each degree you raise or lower the thermostat, heating or cooling costs will be reduced by three to five percent.

• Heating water consumes a lot of energy. Consider installing a water heater blanket around your tank, especially if your water heater is located in an unheated area.

• Drain your water heater periodically to remove sediment and deposits from the bottom of the tank.

• Move the water heater thermostat down to 120 degrees Farenheit. Most water heaters come from the factory set at 140 degrees F. This reduction of 20 degrees can save you about seven percent of your water heater energy cost.

Dedicated to a green lifestyle

• More people are choosing to heat their homes with wood. Get the most efficiency from your wood-burning equipment by cleaning it thoroughly before the start of the season and periodically thereafter. Make sure the intake duct is clear of webs or debris and make sure the chimney is inspected on a regular basis. Use only seasoned wood.

• Close off unused areas of your home. Heat and cool only those rooms that you use.

• Insulate your water pipes. Most water pipes in homes are not insulated, resulting in heat loss, which causes the water heater to work harder. If your pipes are warm to the touch, are "sweaty," or go through unheated areas, the fix is simple and inexpensive. Pre-slit foam pipe insulation is available at most hardware stores. While you're at it, insulate the cold water pipes, too, to prevent them from freezing.

PROBLEM: Wow. After reading all of this, I realize I DO need to consider upgrading my old equipment. Where do I start? *(See also Chapter One: In the Kitchen and Chapter Eleven: At the Office for more energy-saving tips.)* **And what alternative energy sources might become available in the near future?**

I can do that!

• Seek heating and cooling equipment displaying the Energy Star logo. Equipment with this endorsement is guaranteed to be more energy efficient. These products also usually run quieter and have longer lives. Equipment eligible to receive the Energy Star symbol includes boilers, furnaces, heat pumps, programmable thermostats and air conditioners. Many high-efficiency appliances cost more initially, so consider what your savings will be over the life of the appliance.

• Make sure you purchase the correct size system for your living space.

Shades of Green

Takin' it to the next level

• Install a whole-house fan that pulls cool air in and vents warm air through your attic.

• Arrange for an energy audit. A good audit will provide you with a detailed plan for ways you can make improvements, along with estimated energy savings. Audits can be performed by private companies, your utility company or you can even do some audit work online. Then check with your utility to see if it offers incentives or rebates when you make energy-efficient changes. Some do!

• Consider replacing your old windows with double-pane, energy-efficient windows.

• Consider a tankless water heater. These tankless water heaters can deliver as much as 200 gallons of hot water per hour since there is no tank to run out. There is no pilot light and no storage tank of water to keep hot all day—or all night--long. These units only run when you need the hot water, meaning you're no longer paying for standby heat. Different models offer varying water-delivery capacities, they're easy to install and are available in gas or electric models. A tankless system could save as much as 50 percent of your water-heating costs.

• Change what lighting you can to compact fluorescents (CFLs). The up-front cost is high, but you can realize considerable savings. They take longer to warm up but use fewer watts of power for the amount of light generated. They also last longer than the old-fashioned bulbs, which have been around since 1878! Just replace the old bulbs when they blow, if you need to spread the up-front cost over a longer time frame. If one million households changed four light bulbs each, 900,000 tons of greenhouse gases would be eliminated.

Dedicated to a green lifestyle

• Consider energy solutions other than traditional sources, such as natural gas and electricity generated from coal. Electricity today is generated primarily by coal (about 50 percent), followed by nuclear power (19 percent), natural gas (19 percent), hydroelectric (6 percent), petroleum (3 percent) and renewable (2.5 percent). The trend is to look for other ways to produce electricity than by burning fossil fuels -- renewable options.

• Solar power and wind energy are real options now for many parts of the country. You can purchase and install photo voltaic (PV) panels on your roof to generate electricity, while staying connected to your power grid. That way, when there's enough sunlight, your house will be powered primarily by the sun. On dark or rainy days, you still have the traditional power grid to get you by. Some neighborhoods in California have joined forces and purchased PV panels in bulk by forming a community collective.

• Install your own windmill. There are companies out there today eager to help you choose, install and maintain your very own windmill. Your average wind speed should be about 10 miles an hour to make it work for you. Wind can't carry your whole load, but it can go a long way.

• Consider a geothermal heat pump. Geothermal systems use the Earth's temperature a few feet below the surface, which stays fairly consistent all year long. Depending on your latitude, that temperature is between 45 and 75 degrees. A geothermal heat pump brings water up through pipes sunk into the ground. When the outside air is cooler, the water absorbs the Earth's heat. In the summer, the system acts as a heat sink, taking heat from your home's ambient air into the cooler ground. This system can be pricey to install and it doesn't work well in extreme climates. But check for energy rebates and other incentives.

• Don't leave nuclear power off your list of options for someday. Many states have operating nuclear plants, although no new plants are currently being planned. But don't assume the value of nuclear power won't be debated again…in fact it already is getting a second look as a possible short-term solution to the global warming situation. But the jury is still out.

• Biomass and methane are now being used to heat water and generate electricity on a small scale. Methane is created when waste decomposes and is plentiful in landfills. Several states are experimenting with generating electricity from methane gas. And some utilities are already using this technology to produce a small, but growing, portion of the electricity they generate.

• Truly dedicated to a green lifestyle? Get off the grid completely. Some homes have been able to disconnect from the grid by using solar and/or wind power while practicing serious conservation practices.

Chapter Seven:
The Automobile

OK, here we go. The all-American pastime – driving our cars. While a small portion of us has already moved to hybrids and low impact vehicles, most of us have not. Yet it just isn't has hard as you think to do better. In this chapter we will show you how to do that.

Let's keep in mind that this is one of the most important things we can do to reduce our human impact on the environment. In the U.S., about 20 percent of the greenhouse gas emissions come from cars and light trucks. Of course, this contributes significantly to climate change through global warming. It also contributes to air pollution (ask anyone who lives in Los Angeles!), ground pollution as particulate matter is washed out of the air and into our soil, and to disease and medical conditions suffered by many.

If you want to do something to impact the footprint we are making on the environment, this is it. Look at your car, and the use of your car, and start making changes.

PROBLEM: Fossil fuels are the main source of greenhouse emissions we can control. How can we reduce those emissions?

Shades of Green

I can do that!

• Start by simply driving less by driving smarter. Make it a goal to drive 10 miles less each week by combining your trips to the store, shopping and the dry cleaners. Saving 10 miles a week results in a savings of 520 miles a year. That's a significant saving in air emissions and, by the way, you'll save about $225 in gas costs over that same year.

• Don't idle the car to warm it up. First, it's not necessary for today's cars, and second, you don't spew more emissions into the atmosphere while going nowhere.

• Keep your engine tuned up. The difference between a properly tuned engine and one that is not can run from 15 to 50 percent in fuel efficiency!

• Keep your tires at the right pressure. Check monthly, because the average tire loses about one pound per square inch each month. Tires that are under inflated produce drag, lowering fuel efficiency. They wear out faster too. Keeping your tires properly inflated could save you about a tank of gas a year.

• Drive sensibly. Stay off the gas pedal. Jackrabbit starts cost gas mileage. Speeding above 55 mph costs gas mileage. Aggressive driving with lots of acceleration and deceleration costs gas mileage. Here's an example: at 55 mph you will use 15-percent less fuel than at 65 mph. Aggressive driving increases fuel consumption by up to 33 percent! It also results in five times more exhaust emissions than normal driving.

• Don't drive at high speeds with the windows down. This causes drag and reduces fuel efficiency. In fact, go ahead and use that air conditioner. It's actually more fuel efficient than opening the windows (at high speed).

• Don't keep the car loaded down with "stuff." Every extra 100 pounds of stuff will reduce your fuel efficiency by 2 percent.

• Gas. Buy the cheap stuff. Unless you experience problems with regular gas, or your owner's manual specifically requires it, your car was manufactured to run efficiently on 87 octane. Don't go for the 92 octane premium. You will get no improvements to fuel efficiency, engine power, speed or performance. But the price is usually about 20 cents per gallon higher. Save that 20 cents and let it add up. Then buy a hybrid car.

Takin' it to the next level

• It's a lifestyle change, but consider car pooling. Find people at your office or around your neighborhood who work in the same area and set up a car pool. If you cut down just one trip a week, you'll save one-fifth of your gas expenditure, carbon emissions, etc. And money.

• Try telecommuting if your company or business will allow that. Working from home saves you the trip. Sell the idea to your boss as not only green, but more efficient. Remember, you can always go to the office when necessary. Any number of trips to the office you save is a positive step. Think this won't save anything? The average rush-hour commute in 2000 was 62 hours a year! What a waste of time!

• Use mass transit. Use the bus instead of driving. If your city has light rail or subway, use it. It will end up being significantly cheaper than driving even though you still have to pay for the ticket. Remember that a 20-

mile round-trip commute costs about $2,000 a year in gas alone. Anything less than that is savings. And, you are not spewing emissions into the atmosphere. Even if you have to drive a short distance to a bus or rail stop there are still significant savings involved.

• This one will surprise you. If you have a reasonably efficient car now, keep it longer. It actually costs four tons of carbon emissions and almost 700 pounds of other pollutants spewed into the atmosphere to manufacture just one new car!

• Consider biodiesel if your car has a diesel engine. It's renewable, biodegradable, and has none of the sulfur of regular diesel. Biodeisel B20 (a mix of 80-percent conventional diesel and 20-percent biodiesel; biodiesel comes in ranges of B5 to B100, with the higher the number signifying the higher the biofuel content; B20 is the base at which realistic fuel economy savings begin) saves 50 gallons of oil per year and will reduce your carbon emissions by 30 percent.

• If you drive a normal gas-driven engine, explore E85 ethanol. Made from corn and other renewable resources, ethanol can be used by many modern, flex-fuel engines. There are millions on the road now and you may have one and not know it. Ask you dealer.

• Get a different car. Find the highest mileage vehicle you can that has a flex-fuel engine and buy it. Use it for most of your commuting and errands. Cut your emissions and your fuel costs dramatically.

• Get a really different car. Go for a hybrid. These vehicles get excellent mileage and have very low emission rates. Yes, they are a little more expensive, but you'll get that back in fuel efficiency. If you can't do the hybrid, find a small car with a high-mile-per-gallon rating.

• Get a dramatically different car. Look into AFVs (alternative fuel vehicles) or NGVs (natural gas vehicles). Many companies are switching to them for their fleet cars and trucks. The great weakness with these vehicles is the lack of fueling stations. Most of these vehicles are converted from regular gas engines. There are some tax incentives for the purchase of some AFVs and some states allow use of HOV (high-occupancy) lanes for these vehicles.

• If you live and work in an area where you don't have to use major highways to get to and from work, consider a scooter or moped. They cost under $10,000 (and that's for a plush number) but get 50 miles to the gallon or better. They're not great for cold or rainy weather, but fine if you live in a warm climate.

• At your next oil change or service, ask for re-refined motor oil. Producing five quarts of re-refined lubricating oil uses only two gallons of used oil. Producing and refining five quarts of new oil takes two barrels of crude oil. Re-refined motor oil is just fine for your car. If only 5 percent of cars used re-refined oil at every oil changes we would save 2.5 billion gallons of oil a year!

Dedicated to a green lifestyle

• Haven't gone hybrid yet. Do it!

• Dump the car! OK, maybe not, but strongly consider keeping it parked and using it only for special occasions or for trips you can't make any other way. Use public transportation. Walk or ride a bike.

Shades of Green

¤ Consider walking to places that are reasonably close. Really. You'll get exercise—that's good for you--and you'll save gas and emissions, too

¤ Ride that bike to the local stores and nearby shopping.

¤ Use the bus or other public transportation to the mall.

¤ Share shopping trips with neighbors instead of going it alone. Then one vehicle is used instead of two – or three – or more.

• Move. Yes, move to a location closer to work – like walking-distance close. Then use the car only when you have to. And you can more easily use some of the ideas in the point above.

• Campaign for new technologies. Write your Senator and Congressperson to support hydrogen fuel cell technology. It's out there and it's coming. Let's get it done sooner, not later! If not hydrogen, push for electric cars. The technology is improving steadily.

Chapter Eight:
Recycling

Recycling—it's a noble thing to do. And it's getting harder and harder to tell people—maybe even your kids—that you don't recycle. The truth is, though, if it's inconvenient it's a deal breaker. Done well, it doesn't require much time or effort and it sure can make a big difference for you and the environment. However, the national recycling rate is only about 30 percent, according to the EPA. Let's face it—most folks won't drive across town with a car full of recyclable items just to make their contribution to the cause. But more and more community and city leaders are taking a proactive stance and have pushed through local initiatives like curb-side recycling and established drop-off points. And there's every reason to believe the trend will continue.

So, join the cause, learn what to do and get your house recycling program going. Hopefully, this chapter will make it even easier for you than you think. Go at your own pace, but get movin'! The time has come for many people to do some things rather than for one person to do many things. Whatever you do will make a difference.

PROBLEM: I know my day-to-day activities produce materials that I should recycle. But I'm just not sure what to recycle and what to just throw away. I know there must be some guidelines and maybe even some rules. HELP!

Shades of Green

I can do that!

• The first thing you need to do is "think recycling." Energy savings do add up. For instance, it takes 95 percent less energy to produce an aluminum can from recycled aluminum than than from bauxite ore. It takes 40 percent less energy to make a glass bottle from recycled glass than it does to make one from sand, soda ash and limestone. An added bonus? Recycling means less littering.

• The second thing you need to do is understand the entire recycling loop. It's just not enough to send items away to be recycled. You must also purchase recycled products or the process just doesn't work. Read the packaging and do your homework and you can find recycled products and materials.

• Now you're ready to recycle. Set up containers for the following recyclable classes of items: paper and cardboard; plastics; glass; and metals.

• Let's talk paper and cardboard first, since paper takes up about 50 percent of all landfill space. Newspapers should really be saved in its own container as newspapers go directly into newsprint recycling. Recycling a four-foot stack of newspapers saves one 40-foot fir tree! Corrugated cardboard is a highly valued recyclable. But please keep it dry. Plastic or waxy coated cardboard, such as pizza boxes, cannot be recycled.

• Magazines, glossy paper, envelopes, phone books, computer paper and paper packaging can be saved together in one bin. Paper with staples still attached is okay, but remove all rubber bands and plastic overwrap.

Shades of Green

• Plastic—Since it doesn't break down in a landfill and it's a great recyclable item from which many products can be made, try to recycle all plastic waste. But not all plastics are created equal. Plastics #1 and #2 are used for things like milk jugs, liquid detergent and plastic soft drink bottles. Most recyclers want you to rinse these containers out and remove the lids. Lids are not recyclable and should be put in your trash. Plastic #5 is the least recyclable and is used for packaging items such as cottage cheese, margarine and vitamins. These containers may have more value for you to reuse than recycle. So how do I know the number of my plastic item? The number should be stamped on the container, often on the bottom.

• Glass is recycled according to color—clear, green and brown. Most recycling centers prefer donated glass separated by color. It's OK to leave the paper labels on the glass, but you should rinse the bottles and put the lids in the trash. But not all glass is created equal. Light bulbs, Pyrex and mirrors, for example, have a different composition from glass bottles and will be accepted for recycling. These items just shouldn't be mixed in with regular glass items.

• Last, but not least, are the metals—aluminum, steel and copper. Everything from aluminum cans to car engines can be recycled. Aluminum cans, foil and foil packaging are all recyclable items. Paint cans and aerosol cans are recyclable, but the former contents are considered hazardous. So be sure to leave the labels on paint and aerosol cans so recyclers know what used to be in there. Copper is one of the most recyclable of all the metals. In fact, it's 100 percent recyclable. Since bronze and brass are alloys, they're totally recyclable, too.

• Go through the house and find all those pairs of old glasses and sunglasses and donate them to a local charity that distributes them to less fortunate people. If you don't know where to donate them, simply call a local optometrist who should be able to hook you up with an organization or take your old glasses for you.

Dedicated to a green lifestyle

• If your community doesn't have its own recycling program, you can still do your part and organize your neighbors to recycle. Set a specific day each week that someone collects and takes items to a drop-off center.

• Check with your area utilities to see if they currently participate in or plan to have waste-to-energy power generation. A waste-to-energy power plant incinerates garbage and uses the heat to generate steam and produce electricity. It's costly to build one of these plants, but environmentalists believe these facilities will gain popularity as the landfill issue worsens.

PROBLEM: I like to recycle and do a pretty good job of it. But I keep thinking there may be things I can do to reduce the amount of stuff to be recycled in the first place. How can I reduce what comes into my house... and my life? And are there ways to just redistribute all the goods on the planet instead of making more?

I can do that!

• If you haven't done so already, be sure to read Chapter Two about foods and packaging. It contains many tips on how to reduce food waste and unnecessary packaging. Environmentalists have estimated that the average person in the U.S. produces more than four pounds of trash per day. That translates to an average of 1,500 pounds of trash per person each year. If you try, you may be able to recycle up to 70 percent of this waste.

• Before you make any purchase, do the "needs-versus-wants test." It's just too easy today to "buy things" whether you really need them or not. Save your budget, save the planet and learn to be a good consumer. And, if you do decide to make a purchase, go for quality over quantity, buy only from conscientious companies and find out if the products were made with sustainable practices. We have gotten used to being a throwaway society, but we may have to change our thinking.

• Before you go shopping, make a list and then stick to it. This may help you avoid impulse and unnecessary purchases.

• Think about what your purchase may displace. For example, did you buy a new toaster even though your other one still works? If so, why? When the purchase of a new item is necessary, always ask yourself if the old one can be recycled or donated.

• Avoid disposable batteries and make the switch to rechargeable ones. Go even further and buy a solar-powered recharger.

• Send e-cards instead of paper ones. This saves you paper and money.

• Buy products like condiments, liquids and cleaning products in large quantities instead of in smaller sizes to reduce packaging that you just have to throw away anyway. And most times, purchasing in bulk is less expensive.

• Have reusable food storage containers on hand for leftovers and wean off the plastic storage bags.

Takin' it to the next level

• Rent, borrow, trade or pass along things like tools, DVDs and books. It just doesn't make sense to purchase a tool you may use only infrequently. And, most times, we just watch a movie or read a book one time. These things take up valuable space.

• Coordinate with your friends and neighbors to swap baby clothing. The average amount a family spends on clothing and other things for a new baby the first year is more than $5,000! That's crazy when you stop to think about it. Really give some thought to how much baby clothing you should buy new that first year, considering babies change sizes about every three months.

• Now think the same way about adult clothing. There is no better way to save resources and fend off clothes clutter than to buy clothes someone else isn't wearing anymore. Plus, the work has been done and the energy has been spent. Today consignment stores are everywhere...and they are lucrative.

• Reduce the amount of junk mail and catalogues that come into your home. Many states have programs where you can sign up to get yourself removed from junk mail lists. If you have time, you can call vendors who send unsolicited catalogues and ask that your name be removed from their mailings lists. It's so easy today to find desired items and order them online. You don't need the paper catalogue and neither does the environment.

• Stop subscribing to those magazines and newspapers that you probably don't have time to read, anyway. Or coordinate with neighbors, friends and co-workers to share a subscription and route the magazines.

• You can always recycle your phone books, but you can take things a step further by calling to stop your phone book delivery altogether. Today, there are good online phone directories available. It will make a difference, considering telephone books make up almost 10 percent of waste at dump sites.

Dedicated to a green lifestyle

• Don't accept paper and plastic bags from grocers and retailers and bring your own reusable shopping bags with you. That way, you don't have to deal with the extra bags that come into your home and you might save a tree or two along the way. Plus, the landfill has enough plastic bags to last a lifetime…or two…or three.

• When buying gifts for people, think consumable and useful! Give food items, movie tickets, vegetable plants, or even a homemade coupon for baby-sitting or help cleaning. Most people have been given too many things that serve no purpose or are just more knickknacks to dust.

• Mend, fix, reupholster, update and refinish! Many items still have life left in them if you're willing to invest a little time and effort.

Shades of Green

PROBLEM: I like how it feels to recycle and I'm getting the hang of reducing the amount of trash I bring into my home. But now, I am getting the urge to purge...my house, that is! As I begin to sift through the basement, the attic, the crawl space, the garage and all my stuffed closets, what is the right thing to do with what I am willing to part with? Most of it is expired or useless and some things could be harmful for the environment. So it just sits...

I can do that!

• Get rid of all those extra clothes! Someone once said that we wear 20 percent of our clothes 80 percent of the time. Rings true, right? So, be honest and pull those clothes from your closets that you know you have not worn in the last two years. Then give some thought to how many people could use them. High-end items might be appropriate for a consignment shop. That's great. But for most of your clothes, look for worthy charities in your area and make donations. You won't miss what you let go of and you'll feel good about the people you will help. The planet has enough clothes—spread 'em around.

• Plan a garage or yard sale. Think big and make it a larger neighborhood or family garage sale. Set goals for what you'll do with the money and know, in advance, how you will dispose of what doesn't sell. Don't bring things back into the house once the sale is over. Take it all right to your charity of choice.

Takin' it to the next level

• Take the time and effort to try to sell or donate many

of the items you no longer want. In our desire to de-clutter our lives, we must be conscious of what would happen if we all took everything we were discarding to the dump. There are people out there who need what you no longer want. Take the time to find them. Let the Internet work for you and find homes for those things you no longer want. You know what they say—one person's trash is another person's treasure.

• Be responsible when getting rid of things like old batteries, pesticides, chemicals and other hazardous materials. Find out where to take these items and never put them in your regular trash.

Dedicated to a green lifestyle

• We all have obsolete computers and computer components, televisions and cell phones in our homes. And, if you're willing to take the time, you might be able to find good homes for these items. Many school, churches and non-profit organizations have a need for working computers. Some women's shelters welcome cell phones. But getting rid of these items safely is becoming a real nightmare on a global scale. There are between 300,000 to 400,000 tons of electronics collected for recycling in the U.S. each year. And activists report that more than half ends up overseas in countries like China, Nigeria and India. Workers there dismantle these electronics by hand, exposing them and the environment to toxic chemicals. So, before you take your electronics for recycling, ask the tough questions and find out where these items are going, as more U.S. landfills are banning this type of waste. There may soon come a day when U.S. manufacturers will be required to take back and recycle their own equipment. If that happens, manufacturers will begin making their products with fewer toxic chemicals, which will make them easier to recycle.

• Remember that when we "throw away" items, there really is no "away." All of our trash ends up somewhere—in our land, air, water or in living things—that means in us, too. Landfills are reaching capacity and it's becoming harder to find new sites for landfills. Incineration, another alternative to landfills, has its own problems in terms of producing highly toxic residue ash. And guess what? That ash has to be taken away and put somewhere—like in a landfill. Think globally by giving thought to where your trash is going. Just because it's out of your sight doesn't mean it's really out of your life and the lives of your family.

Chapter Nine:
Water Conservation

Water is THE absolute necessity of life. We cannot survive as a species or as a planet without it. We use water everywhere. In the house. Out of the house. Around the house. At the office. Everywhere. Yet in many parts of the country, water is becoming more and more precious and expensive. And while it's renewable, we still have to clean it to use it. And in many parts of the country it's more and more difficult to obtain. In this chapter we demonstrate how to save water or use less of it.

If you haven't experienced a water shortage yet, you will. We waste clean water at a prodigious rate. Did you know that about one-third of the water we use during the summer goes on grass – not to people? In the average large city we use 50 to 75 million gallons of water a day just to water our grass. Yet a few states away, water is scarce.

Did you know that most of the world gets by on only 2.5 gallons of water a day per person? In the United States, however, the average person uses 400 gallons a day! Yet even in this country, Florida is experiencing fresh water shortages and they are common as well in the Southwest. Experts agree that if we don't get a handle on this simple problem, some cities will be importing water within 20 years. Los Angeles already has to import water to support its population. Las Vegas is a water sponge as well.

Shades of Green

PROBLEM: We use far too much water in the house for routine activities such as washing, using the toilet, bathing, etc. I can make some differences simply by changing habits. And, I can lower my water bill every month besides!

I can do that!

In the bathroom:

• Here's a simple one: just turn off the water while you are brushing your teeth! While that toothbrush and toothpaste is doin' its thing, running water accomplishes nothing other than wasting water. Just turn off the water while you brush, then turn it back on to rinse. Water companies suggest the savings from this simple action alone will amount to seven gallons a minute!

• Do the same while you are shaving. Turn off the water while slicing off that hair, then turn it on again to rinse. Another seven gallons per minute!

• Check your sink and toilet for leaks. A leaking toilet can use 90,000 gallons of water in just one month. Fix as necessary.

• Check your faucet for drips. A dripping faucet can waste as much as 20 gallons a day! Fix as necessary.

• Take shorter showers. Reducing your time in the shower by just a few minutes can save 20 to 30 gallons of water each day.

• If you like baths, fill the tub half-full instead of completely full. You will still get clean and save up to 4,500 gallons of water a year.

Shades of Green

• Flush less. During the California drought many operated on the following principle: "When it's brown, flush it down; when it's yellow, let it mellow." They cut their water usage significantly. You can too.

• Don't use the toilet as a trash can. Throw waste in the trash can, not the toilet. If it smells, take in outside.

In the kitchen:

• Save that dish for tomorrow. Not everything has to be cleaned right after use (my drill sergeant is cringing right now). Batch your dishes to wash them in a group and get some efficiencies in your water usage.

• Don't use the dishwasher unless you can fill the machine.

In the laundry:

• Wash full loads only! Practice a little patience and wait for that favorite shirt one more day until you have a full load.

• Use the right water level on your washing machine. It should just cover your clothing in the basket when fully loaded. Anything more is wasted.

Takin' it to the next level

In the bathroom:

• Install a low-flow shower head. This simple action that costs less than $30 can save as much as five gallons of water a minute.

Shades of Green

• Install faucet aerators on your faucets. They cost pennies and deliver as strong a flow as without them. But, they can reduce your water use as much as 50 percent!

• Make certain your water heater is the right size for your family. Water heaters store water to match your peak needs. If you have downsized recently, you may not need the larger heater. If that's the case, replace it. They last less than 10 years these days anyway.

In the kitchen:

• Install a new, water-efficient dishwasher. These new dishwashers, although more expensive, use significantly less water than older machines.

• Or…wash your own dishes and get rid of the dishwasher all together! Washing by hand uses less water.

In the laundry:

• Install new, water-efficient clothes washing machines. These new machines use up to 35 percent less water than conventional machines. Some don't even use water! Sanyo makes a new machine that uses ozone instead of water to clean your clothes.

Dedicated to a green lifestyle

In the bathroom:

• Install a new, low-flow toilet. These new toilets use only 1.6 gallons per flush instead of 3.5 to 7 gallons for older toilets. You can cut your water usage by as much as 20 percent just with this one action. That means a family of four saves 4,000 gallons of water a year!

• There are now new systems that allow you to use the water from the tank refilling to wash your hands after using the toilet. That's using the water twice.

In the kitchen:

• Knock off the bottled water! Instead, install a simple water filter on your faucets. A water filter can cost as little as $30. That equals about a month's worth of bottled water. How does this help? It saves tons of plastic used to store that bottled water, much of which ends up in landfills. And, it's not biodegradable!

• If you are ready, and zoning laws allow, dig a well if your water table will support one. You'll use your own assets, not strain the local water system, and cut your water bill to zero.

In the laundry:

• Harvest your "grey water." Grey water is water that has been used for things like sinks, dish washing, showers and clothes washing. It's not sewage water from the toilet; that's called "black water." Grey water can be recycled with new plumbing systems for use in the garden, on the lawn, etc. There are now new systems designed to do just this sort of thing.

• Think about where you live. If you live in a dry area, and are ready or able to move, do so. Select a location more suited to human habitation where your presence will not significantly impact the water table.

PROBLEM: We waste a lot of water outside our homes, watering lawns and gardens. Taking simple actions can save water usage significantly. Save money too.

Shades of Green

I can do that!

• Most lawns need to be watered only an hour a week. Limit your grass watering to just that.

• If you get into a drought situation, remember that most lawn grass can survive dormant for up to six weeks.

• If you use an irrigation system, and these can be very efficient, make sure you install a rain sensor that tells the system when to water and when not to (as in, it's raining!). Depending on your climate, you could save as much as 30 percent of your water usage per year.

• Always use a mulching lawnmower. The grass clippings are returned to the lawn as fertilizer and the clippings actually serve as mulch for the lawn to help it retain water in hot, sunny weather.

• Avoid watering your lawn during the heat of the day to prevent evaporation. Water in the early morning or early evening.

• Don't hose down outside equipment or the driveway. Use a broom rather than water. It's cheaper and will save water.

• Don't use water to wash your car at home. Commercial car washes are more efficient with their use of water and usually have to meet strict recycling and waste quality standards. You can't compete and you can't do it as efficiently as they can.

Takin' it to the next level

• Install an automatic shut-off nozzle on your garden

hose to prevent waste when the water is on and the hose is not in use.

• Install a drip irrigation system for your flower beds and garden. The simple investment in a drip or soaker hose can save up to 70 percent of the water you would normally use.

• If you have a swimming pool, cover it when you are not using it. Without a cover, evaporation alone will cost you 90 percent of your water.

• Replace water intensive and needy plantings with hardier plants that can withstand dry conditions more readily. Target plants native to your region of the country that need little or no watering, not water intensive imports.

• Stop the extensive use of fertilizers. What does this have to do with water? Best estimates are that as much as half of all fertilizers are washed into the local aquifer and then require filtering or treatment before that water can be reused. Fertilize once in the spring and again once in the fall.

Dedicated to a green lifestyle

• Use "grey water" to water exterior plants and landscaping.

• Establish a rainwater collection system and use it for exterior watering, like for your plants and even for your lawn.

• Replace your traditional lawn with water-friendly ground cover.

Shades of Green

• Install a water sprinkler system. The initial expense is much lower if you are under construction. And the system will amortize itself in as little as five years. After that, it's all savings. And you'll be saving water that entire time.

• With new construction, there are many options. Start with rainwater collection systems like cisterns. Build in systems to reuse "grey water."

• As has already been mentioned, dig your own well.

• If you have a swimming pool… well, shut it down. Pools are enormous water users and, in an effort to beat the heat, many are located in water shortage areas. Use a community pool instead.

Chapter Ten:
Outside the House

Every time we go outside we trash the environment. Oh, we're not really trying to do that, we just do it as a consequence of all the normal things we do -- in our garages, on our lawns, our cars and driveways, in our back yards. The products we use work great, but they also leave residue that washes into the water table, add toxic chemicals to the soil, contaminate our air and our plants.

But many of the products or activities we do outside our homes can be replaced with simple – or sometimes not so simple – alternatives that are much friendlier to the environment.

Here we show you how to decrease your impact on the environment through simple good ideas.

PROBLEM: In maintaining our homes, we all too often use toxic chemicals and products that harm the environment. What can we do to move away from these products?

I can do that!

• When it's time to paint, avoid lead-based paints. OK, you knew that. But do you always check the label on the can?

Shades of Green

• When painting exteriors, consider using recycled paint. Yes, there is such a thing, and the quality is just as good as new paint. Using a recycled product will keep paint from going into the landfills (it's often quite toxic), and it actually costs 30 to 50 percent less than new paint.

Takin' it to the next level

• When you replace or rebuild that outdoor deck, don't use wood. Treated lumber takes more trees out of the ecosystem, and the chemicals used to treat the wood are highly toxic to the environment and to humans. Two products today are very environmentally friendly and more durable than wood. One is concrete and the other is composite materials.

• Make sure your house is appropriately insulated for your climate. Newer homes are usually properly insulated today, but older homes (built before 1975) may not be. Get an expert to evaluate your home for insulation. The U.S. Department of Energy and Department of Housing and Urban Development publish good guidelines that are often more stringent than local building codes. We recommend the DOE/HUD guidelines. There's a great online tool for calculating insulation costs at http://rehabadvisor.pathnet.org/. Remember that some upgrades like this are eligible for tax credits.

Dedicated to a green lifestyle

• Replace your roof. Yes, that's expensive, but not if you are building a new house or if your roof is ready for replacement. Just replace it with a light-colored material. Choose recycled materials, of course. Most roofs in the U.S. are dark, and absorb heat during the summer. A light-colored roof will reflect more heat and save you cooling costs--as much as $60 per year for a 2,000-square-foot house. Of course, it also reduces air pollution and greenhouse gas emissions because you are using less energy.

• Replace your roof. Here's an even better idea. Install a highly reflective roofing material. Just this one action can save an average of 1,000 kilowatt-hours of electricity. That's about $90 per year in cooling costs – more than you'll save by turning up your thermostat by three degrees. If only one in a hundred new homes used highly reflective roofs, the total energy savings would be equal to that generated by a solar panel the size of the Pentagon!

• Replace, or use, eco-friendly insulation. It should go without saying that you need insulation in both summer and winter to retain heat and cool. But most of the commercially available insulation today is fiberglass. Fiberglass is not easily biodegradable. but alternatives are, including recycled newspaper, glass, and other recovered insulating materials. The energy used to create these insulation materials is one-sixth that required for fiberglass.

• Replace your windows. If you don't have at least double-paned windows, get them. What kind will depend upon your climate and region of the country. This one act can save up to $400 per year in electricity costs.

• Save some trees. If you are building a new home, tell your builder you want to use recycled wood instead of new wood. Recycled wood mostly comes from wood originally culled from old-growth forests and is actually of higher quality than standard lumber. It can be as much as four times more energy efficient and can last three to four times longer. If you can't get recycled wood, look for wood that has been certified by the Forest Stewardship Council. The council certifies that this wood comes from forests that are properly managed for sustainability – maintaining fragile habitats and water supplies and protecting local communities.

• Select a proper site for your home – one that will be close to your work, shopping and schools so you can minimize your driving. If you choose a site that saves just one mile a day, you would save, on average, 500 miles per year. That equates to about 20 gallons of gas on the average car, at $3 per gallon or $60.00 per year in your pocket. If one in 10 of us did that, we would save as much as 2.4 million gallons a year! This reduces air pollution and cost by as much as $7.2 million.

• When building, consider proper site selection. Look for a north-south orientation for your front and back where most of the windows are located. You'll get good sunlight during the winter, but not that direct afternoon sunlight that a westerly exposure will provide. Just avoiding the westerly exposure can save as much as 25 percent on your cooling bill during the summer.

Editors' Note: The National Association of Home Builders has already established National Green Home Building Guidelines. You can get those free by visiting www.nahb.com.

These guidelines include six primary areas: Lot Preparation and Design; Resource Efficiency; Energy Efficiency; Water Efficiency and Conservation; Occupancy Comfort and Indoor Environmental Quality; and Home Owner Guidance on How to Optimally Operate and Maintain the House. Get a copy before talking to your builder.

In addition, the NAHB has created a National Green Building Standard for all builders. This standard is currently available on their website at http://www.nahbgreen.org/.

PROBLEM: My swimming pool might be an environmental problem. It uses lots of water and I have to use chlorine to purify the water. What can I do?

I can do that!

• Start by covering your pool when it's not in use. You'll cut water lost to evaporation by 90 percent. The average uncovered pool will lose about 1,000 gallons of water a month. That much water will take care of an average family of four for more than a year! Cover your pool with a pool cover or a tarp to save water. You'll also save money since you will not have to replace the water lost by evaporation.

• Stop with the chlorine already! The EPA classifies chlorine as a pesticide. It's been liked to asthma, lung damage, allergies and other health problems. Belgium has already banned the use of chlorine in public swimming pools.

• Replace chlorine with more environmentally, and healthy, alternatives. Some are fairly simple, others require more investment. Here are a few of the simpler alternatives:

¤ Try Chlorfree Ionizing Capsules. These are

capsules you immerse in your pool. They are filled with copper, zinc, palladium, silver and carbon. When exposed to water, they create an ionization effect to kill bacteria, algae, microbes and other such bad stuff. There are no other filters to use so they use little energy. Just these capsules alone can reduce your chlorine use by 85 percent.

¤ Try attaching an ozone generator to your existing pool filtration system. These generators pump ozone gas into the water which forms oxygen that neutralizes bacteria, viruses, algae and others agents the same way chlorine does. While they still require some chlorine use, they reduce it by 80 percent.

Takin' it to the next level

• Install a new filtration system in your pool that uses salt to filter the water. Much like home systems, salt turns into small amounts of chlorine and cleans the water, which is then recycled into the system. The chlorine is then recycled back into salt. These systems take an investment, require salt replenishment and also have a learning curve to get the PH values set appropriately, but are very efficient and effective once up and running. And they use no chlorine additives.

Dedicated to a green lifestyle

• Let's start with finding out why you need a swimming pool. It consumes huge quantities of a precious resource – water. If you have a community pool, consider not using yours, or even replacing it with a garden – or a wildlife habitat.

• If you must have a pool, try a natural swimming pool system. This type of pool is becoming very popular in Europe. This involves using plants and special micro-organisms to mimic the natural filtration that takes place in nature. The water is clean but not pure, but much like swimming in a mountain stream or a freshwater pond. It is expensive to build, but is self cleaning and requires no chemicals and no filters. Just maintain the plants. Here's a link for more info: http://www.motherearth-news.com/Do-It-Yourself/2002-08-01/Natural-Swim-ming-Pool.aspx.

PROBLEM: Lawn care takes a lot of time, energy, and cost. Are there some good, green alternatives that will save me time, money and are environmentally appropriate?

I can do that!

• Use a mulching lawnmower blade. Mulching blades let you leave the grass clippings on the lawn. They serve as a mulch to help retain moisture in the lawn, reducing the amount of water your lawn needs. It also reduces bagging and raking efforts and reduces waste that must be removed and disposed of. All this saves energy. And, sun and air will break down the clippings into fertilizer for your lawn. (The EPA estimates that 31 million tons of yard waste is collected and processed annually in the U.S.)

• Cut your grass a little higher. The best height is two and a half inches. This provides a good-looking lawn, but reduces the number of times you have to cut it. It allows the grass longer roots (there is a direct relationship between grass height and length of roots) allowing the grass to establish itself better, seek water more deeply and require less watering. The reduced number of mowings alone will save significantly on air pollution.

• Keep your mower blades sharp. Dull blades damage grass by tearing them rather than cutting them. They then require more water than healthy grass.

• Keep your mower in good shape. Make sure it's running well.

• If you must use fertilizer, forget the old moniker EMIL (Easter, May Day, Independence Day, and Labor Day). Most lawn professionals (those not trying to sell you services!) suggest that only an early fertilizing in the spring and a final one in the fall are necessary.

• If you get into a drought, don't over water your grass. If it begins to turn brown, that's a natural function of the grass protecting itself. Don't trade severe loss of water for a green lawn. It's not worth the natural resource.

• Water your grass only about one hour each week. Make sure you water in the early morning or late evening to avoid evaporation loss. Lawn watering is the number one problem during droughts. Outdoor lawn watering makes up about 40 percent of household water bills during the summer! We use about 7.9 billion gallons of water a day just for our lawns! What a waste of a precious natural resource.

• Use pesticides sparingly. In the U.S., we seriously overuse pesticides with dangerous consequences to our environment. Yes, they are sometimes necessary. When they are, look for Green Chemistry pesticides and follow instructions to the letter to protect your environment. The chemical industry is developing more environmen-

Shades of Green

tally friendly pesticides so look for these.

Takin' it to the next level

• Replace your lawnmower with an electric mower. There are several excellent models now available. These include new battery-operated mowers with light engines and bodies that make them easy to push.

• Forget fertilizer. Especially avoid fertilizing only to green your lawn. Most lawns get far more nitrates (that's what turns grass green) from natural sources anyway.

• Stay away from using other chemicals on you lawn unless you absolutely have to do so. Many of these chemicals wash residue into the water table and contaminate our water, and they are also harmful to wildlife.

• As you reseed each year, consider replacing your grass with native varieties that are disease and drought resistant. Bluegrasses are good, but take a lot of water. Rye grasses are better.

• If you must water your lawn, consider a lawn irrigation system with a rain sensor. Irrigation systems, while a little costly, allow you to control the water flow quite precisely to the right amount – and not more. And the installation of a rain sensor insures that you don't have your system watering the grass while it rains!

• Instead of using weed killers and pre-emergents, consider doing it the old fashioned way. Weed by hand once a week. There are even some very good tools available to make it easier today. This keeps more harmful chemicals out of the soil and water.

• Put containers under your rainwater downspouts to

catch and hold rainwater. Then use this water on your lawn, plants and garden. It's perfectly good water and you'll save on straining your local water supply.

Dedicated to a green lifestyle

• Mow your lawn with a manual reel lawnmower instead of a gas or electric mower. You'll get more exercise and the lawn will look just as good. And, you'll save on gas, oil and maintenance. And, most importantly, you will be putting NO pollutants into the air. That's environmentally friendly. These are the mowers your grandparents used. Five percent of the nation's air pollution comes from lawn mower use!

• Reduce (or eliminate) the amount of grass you have. Grass is not a natural ecosystem. We create lawns artificially for appearance. Better, plant ground cover native to your region, plant trees and bushes, and perhaps even vegetables. Grass lawns need a great deal more water than any of these alternatives, and mowing them increases air pollutants. Xeriscaping is now becoming popular. This is the practice of using drought-resistant plants in your lawn and garden. One example is to use clover instead of traditional grass. Clover is drought-resistant, tolerant of weeds and insects and requires minimal lawn mowing. It's attractive and provides a comfortable cushion to walk on.

PROBLEM: Gardens and plantings are very water and pesticide intensive. What alternatives are there?

I can do that!

• Make sure your garden hose is fitted with an automatic shut-off nozzle. This eliminates wasted water when you set the hose down to do something else. In addition, these nozzles allow you to control the rate of water flow so you can use just enough and not too much.

• Stop using gas-powered lawn and garden tools. The EPA estimates they alone account for about 5 percent of the nation's air pollution. Use electric if you must, or better yet, use unpowered tools – people power.

Takin' it to the next level

• Install a drip irrigation system for your plantings and gardens. These are not expensive and allow you to positively control both the amount of water you use and direct it specifically where it is needed. You reduce evaporation significantly and provide the water directly to the plants. You can save as much as 70 percent of the water you usually use with just this one method.

• Plant more shade trees around your house. A good 25- foot shade tree can save you as much as 10 percent of your air-conditioning bill. Plant trees on the west and east sides of the house. Their shade provides significant savings.

Dedicated to a green lifestyle

• Go for complete Xeriscaping of your house. Work with a local landscaper to select drought-tolerant planting materials that are native to your region. Yank all that water hungry stuff out and replace it.

• Use a portion of the back yard for a vegetable and herb garden.

Shades of Green

PROBLEM: What other things can I do outside that might help the environment?

I can do that!

• Exchange your external light bulbs with CFLs (fluorescents). Just this simple action can save you $35 a year in electricity cost for four bulbs. They use 66 percent less energy and last three times longer.

• Connect your external lighting to a light sensor that turns them on and off as lighting conditions suggest. This keeps their usage to a minimum – just when it's dark enough outside to need them.

• Consider solar-powered outdoor lighting. The light it emits is somewhat dull, but the energy costs are free!

Takin' it to the next level

• In the winter, don't idle your car to warm it up. That wastes gas and puts more pollutants into the air. An idling car emits 20 times the pollution than one traveling at 32 miles an hour! If it's cold in the car, wear a coat and gloves. It will warm up soon enough. Manufacturers no longer suggest that cars need a warm-up period.
• Start composting. Compost is recycled food scraps, yard trimmings, paper, ashes from the fireplace, trimmings from bushes and trees. From your composting, you can get natural fertilizers for your garden. You can buy a commercial compost unit at any lawn and garden center or online.

Dedicated to a green lifestyle

• Replace your driveway and walkways with a porous

pavement. These driveways allow for the absorption of rain water instead of having it run off into the sewer system as it does with regular concrete or asphalt driveway materials. Porous pavement also helps with pollutant runoff and sewer overflow problems.

• Instead of wood siding or shingles, replace them with new concrete or composite siding.

Chapter Eleven:
At the Office

This book, so far, has been about how to make our homes more eco-friendly and our existence on the planet less intrusive. But what about those eight to 10 hours a day we spend at the office? There's an opportunity to make a difference, too! Whether or not our employer is environmentally aware, there are things we can all do to be greener in the workplace—maybe bringing our employer along at the same time.

It's easy to think that our employers are the ones responsible for any decisions regarding trash, energy use, water consumption and so on. But the truth is you can make a huge impact on a daily basis. And guess what? You might even make your place of employment one that better attracts and retains employees and lifts morale in the workplace on a daily basis. Becoming environmentally active is a team sport and, these days, many people want to play. Employee buy-in is vital to all the following ideas, so be that cheerleader and get things going.

Here are some simple, and maybe not-so-simple, things you and your co-workers can do to live a greener lifestyle during those hours in the workplace.

Shades of Green

PROBLEM: Did you know commercial buildings use about 18 percent of all the energy in this country? And about one-fourth of that amount is for lighting alone. What are some things individual workers can do to help save energy?

I can do that!

• If you're the last person in an office or common area, turn out the lights. So much of the office electricity is spent lighting offices that are vacant or when there is sufficient natural light to go without overhead lighting. Plus, natural light means less eye fatigue.

• Activate the power management function, or sleep mode, on your computer monitors. You don't need a screen saver.

• Use the "standby" button on your copier and you'll save about 70 percent of that machine's energy load annually.

• Make good use of power strips for your computers, printers, fax machine, scanners and other equipment that has a standby mode. Then, just before you leave your office, simply switch off the power strips.

Takin' it to the next level

• Have your company contact the local utility company and ask for an energy audit. These audits are free or are conducted for a modest fee and can save thousands of dollars. But be sure you understand what you're asking for. A preliminary audit is basically a walk-through by an energy expert that generates a list of recommendations. There are also general audits and investment audits that could mean more company expense at the beginning but a clearly defined and achievable return on investment over time.

• Don't forget the value of your employees. Oftentimes, employees can perform a walk-through inspection and provide ideas for ways to cut costs. Better yet, start a Green Suggestion program, with simple incentives, and see what ideas you get. You might be surprised!

• Encourage your company to be energy efficient with its heating and cooling. This includes regular maintenance, programmable thermostats that employees cannot change and good use of space fans and airflow.

• Remember to occasionally clean the back of the fridge in the employee kitchen for increased efficiency and air circulation.

• When replacing office equipment, make sure your company chooses new equipment with the ENERGY STAR emblem.

• When phasing out older desktop PCs, replace them with laptops. They consume five times less electricity.

Dedicated to a green lifestyle

• Weatherproof your company building by doing things such as increasing insulation, replacing old windows, adding skylights and covering leaky power outlets. For more energy-saving ideas, see Chapter Six.

• Install faucet aerators and low flow toilets to conserve water usage. See Chapter Nine for more water tips.

Shades of Green

• Review your artificial lighting and change bulbs, when possible, to CFLs (compact fluorescent lights). They are more expensive to purchase, but more than make up for it in terms of longer life and reduced energy use.

• If your company is building a new office or adding on to or renovating an existing one, encourage the use of green building materials and designs. Companies can receive certifications for green buildings, which is great public relations and serves as a great example for other businesses. And employees will be proud of the effort, too.

• Ask your utility company if you can purchase green power, power they may generate or buy that is created from renewable energy sources such as wind, hydro-power or landfill gas.

• If your company is large enough, suggest the hiring of a person dedicated to promoting energy savings. An employee hired to promote energy conservation can save the company a lot of money and help advance its eco-friendly goals. This person can work with local utilities and energy experts to find major savings in areas such as heating, air conditioning, lighting and water usage. If not an employee, contract with an expert.

PROBLEM: There is so much waste in an office environment. I don't set office policies regarding what types of supplies we order or how things are disposed of. And the office kitchen is certainly not in my job responsibilities. What can I do?

Shades of Green

I can do that!

• The average office worker uses about 10,000 sheets of copy paper in a year. For the entire country, that's four trillion sheets! Every time you go to make copies, think about how many copies of something you truly need.

• And, when possible, make two-sided copies. It is estimated that about 750,000 copies are made every minute nationwide during the average work day. Every 100 reams of recycled office paper that is printed double-sided saves two trees. You could also set each copier so that the duplex printing mode is the default.

• Use postconsumer recycled paper. In fact, there are recycled or organic versions of many office supplies, from copy paper to sticky notes to refillable pens.

• Give paper a second life. Beyond recycling it, consider what else you might be able to do with it. How about using the blank side for notes? Or maybe take the paper home and let your kids color on the blank side. Some companies shred a lot of scrap paper and then use as packing material for shipping fragile items.

• Re-use file folders. Simply turn them inside out and re-label.

• Use inkjet printers instead of laser printers. Laser printers use 3 times the electricity.

• That brings us to the subject of toner cartridges for printers and copiers. If you consistently make fewer copies, it stands to reason that you'll save ink as well as paper. And, when you do need to change toner cartridges, make sure your company participates in a recycling program.

Shades of Green

- You can refill and reuse ink cartridges, too.

- Use postconsumer recycled envelopes and reuse them as many times as you can.

- Green your printing. Select vendors who use recycled papers and soy-based inks.

- When faxing, avoid using a cover page when you can. Better yet, fax from your computer and don't use any paper on your end at all. Better yet, don't fax. Scan and email instead.

- Reuse your paper clips and binder clips—so many are thrown away because workers don't take the time to pull them off. Enough new paper clips are made each year to hand every American at least three. Simply put—the planet has enough paper clips. Reuse them!

- Don't waste food, napkins, ketchup packets and other things in your company kitchen or cafeteria. Take only what you need—not a handful of napkins and condiment packets. It all adds up.

- Reduce the number of newspaper and magazine subscriptions and do a better job of routing issues or placing them in common areas.

Takin' it to the next level

- Ask your boss or purchasing department to buy recycled paper for the copiers and printers.

Shades of Green

• Choose suppliers who take back their packaging for reuse. And make sure you communicate your green goals to all vendors and suppliers.

• Get rid of the notion that every employee has to have a printer. Buy and maintain fewer printers by placing them in centralized locations.

• When printing a document that is not yet final, print it in draft mode. Draft mode uses less ink. There is also software available that allows you to control the amount of ink a printer uses.

• Try printing online stamps instead of using a postage meter. You'll save on equipment and ink.

• See if you can convince your company to abandon Styrofoam and plastic cups, utensils and other disposable cafeteria supplies. And bring your own china or ceramic coffee mug to work and use that every day. Styrofoam takes nine generations to biodegrade.

• Insist on permanent cloth or mesh coffee filters instead of disposable paper filters for your common-area coffee makers.

• Coordinate an office recycling program for paper, toner cartridges and other items. Oftentimes a company will get on board as long as employees are willing to manage it. If you can't get a recycling program going company wide, at least recycle your own paper and supplies.

• Recycling efforts tend to be more successful if there is an appointed recycling coordinator. Volunteer to be that person.

Shades of Green

• Create a green team of employees from all divisions of your organization to bring new ideas to the forefront.

Dedicated to a green lifestyle

• Avoid rubber bands. Most rubber bands are synthetic, made from crude oil.

• Use an eco-stapler, which does not use metal staples. They work great for stapling up to five pages, which accounts for most of our office stapling tasks. For documents containing more than five pages, use a paper clip or binder clip and then recycle those clips again and again.

• Help your company find great ways to dispose of old computer and office equipment. Most computers being replaced are still fully functioning and would be a great philanthropic gift to a not-for-profit or other worthwhile organization. The same goes for older office furniture.

• Encourage the practice that any trinkets and rewards given by the company to employees, vendors or customers be useful and made out of recycled material. No one needs another unusable trinket that just collects dust and eventually gets thrown away.

• The next time someone suggests a team-building exercise, seek a "green" activity like cleaning a park or planting flowers.

PROBLEM: Part of the waste I see with my company is centered on transportation, business travel and missed opportunities to possibly work from home.

Shades of Green

I can do that!

• Workers drive an average of 10,000 miles a year to and from work. So carpool to work, if possible. Carpooling can save a person about 500 gallons of gasoline a year, not to mention how one less car on the road lessens the impact of exhaust emissions on the environment. Multiply that nationwide! How about incentives for carpoolers, like a prime parking spot?

• Live two miles or less from work? Why not walk or bike to work? You'll save gas money, probably be healthier and help the environment.

• Mass transit is an option, too. Some employers provide tax-advantage spending accounts for employees to cover the cost of riding the bus, train or subway. These programs allow employees to pay for their mass transit expenses with pre-tax dollars.

Takin' it to the next level

• Bring your lunch to work and stay in. Besides the miles it takes to get to and from work, most workers get in their cars and go out to lunch. Bringing your lunch could have added benefits besides gasoline savings— you'll probably save lunch money and eat healthier.

• Do you have the type of job that would allow you to telecommute, even on a part-time basis? Today, about 44 million people work from home at least part of the time. It could be as easy as just asking. An added benefit of telecommuting might also be the need to buy fewer clothes and, consequently, use less dry cleaning.

Shades of Green

• Save time and money by teleconferencing. It's less expensive for the company and much better for the environment to teleconference than put employees on a plane.

• If employees do have to travel for business, you and your boss should make every effort to juggle schedules to possibly make two trips into one.

Dedicated to a green lifestyle

• Encourage your company to green its fleet by buying energy-efficient or hybrid vehicles. This saves money and sets an example at a corporate level.

• Does your company use a lot of courier services? Insist on the use of bicycle couriers for local needs.

Chapter Twelve:
Green Travel

We all travel. We travel for business, for pleasure, for vacations. We use airplanes. We use automobiles. We even use boats and trains. We visit locations. We go to meetings, stay in hotels—or we camp. We visit tourist venues. We eat in restaurants—or take our own food and cook it. Some of us even use recreation vehicles and take our environment with us.

The problem is all this travel can put excessive wear on our environment. In our journeys, we endanger the very places, sights, historical locations and wildernesses we travel to see in the first place. Yet there is much we can do to mitigate our impact on the environment as we travel. It just takes a little thought and effort.

We don't have to endanger our travel locations. We don't have to add to the pollution that chokes our air, our water, our land. Yet we can still travel. We can still enjoy these places. And we can leave these destinations in good condition for the next travelers. And we don't have to sacrifice our comfort or go into the middle of nowhere to be a green traveler.

In this section you will find ideas that others have developed over the years to help you impact our environment as little as possible while you travel. And, along the way, these tips my also enhance your experience, make travel more enjoyable, more educational, and possibly even less expensive.

Shades of Green

PROBLEM: It's easy to waste energy, supplies, water and more when you stay at a hotel.

I can do that!

• Use the same linens and towels in your hotel room throughout your stay. You probably don't change your sheets and towels daily at home, so why do it when you're away? To keep track of which towel belongs to which family member, bring safety pins with different colored beads and designate a color for each person. Be sure to remove the pins when you get ready to leave. Leave a note for housekeeping so they know what you're doing.

• Treat your hotel room like you do your own house. Turn off lights and appliances, including radios and television sets, when leaving your room. And, on the way out, turn back your room thermostat to a lower setting for heating and a higher setting for air conditioning. Also, close the drapes.

• Unplug your chargers and adaptors when they're not in use.

Takin' it to the next level

• Choose only eco-friendly hotels. Look at their marketing materials and see if you can find a clearly stated environmental policy and/or evidence the hotel actively supports local environmental issues.

• Pack your own toiletries instead of relying on hotel supplies. You'll have the brands you want and you'll help create less plastic waste. Leave any unopened toiletry bottles in the room for the next guest.

• Keep bar soap wrappers and take used bars of soap home to use.

• Pack a night light instead of leaving a bathroom light (and possible a bathroom fan) on all night.

• If your hotel provides a complimentary newspaper, pass yours along to someone else, leave it in the lobby for another reader or ask the hotel to see that it's recycled.

• Wait until you get home to wash your clothes. The hotel industry uses 16,863 gallons of water per room per year. An average 150-room hotel uses as many resources in a week as 100 families use in a year.

• Check out by using the hotel room's television, if possible, to help reduce paperwork.

• Always fill out comment cards after your stay to suggest ways management can become more environmentally friendly.

Dedicated to a green lifestyle

• Take, use and refill a single water bottle, thermos or canteen per person when you travel. This way, you can avoid all the plastic bottles that you'd end up throwing away.

• Look for hotels and resorts that use environmentally sensitive, renewable energy, water and waste disposal systems.

Shades of Green

• Find out if your hotel irrigates its lawns and gardens with gray water (water from bath and laundry sources).

• Find out if your hotel uses solar or wind power.

• Find out if your hotel separates trash and composts.

• Find out if your hotel or resort was built with recycled building materials or those harvested in a sustainable manner.

PROBLEM: We sometimes waste resources before we even go on a trip.

I can do that!

• Use a digital camera instead of one that needs film. The solutions used to make prints often contain hazardous chemicals that require special treatment and disposal. So, if you haven't transitioned to digital yet, do it. And avoid using disposable cameras. Despite the claim on the box that they are recycled, more than half end up in the trash.

• Research guidebooks online and only print out the pages you need, as opposed to buying the entire book.

• Use e-tickets instead of printed tickets.

• Use self-service check-in and print-at-home tickets. This saves the airlines money and is less hassle for you. You can print your tickets on recycled paper, where the ones at the airport are harder to recycle because of the inks and, in some cases, a magnetic strip.

Takin' it to the next level

• Use online maps instead of paper maps or use a GPS navigation system. Online maps are free and can be recycled after you've printed them out and used them.

• Take the least amount of luggage possible and carry on what you can. Luggage carousels use lots of energy—not to mention you can reduce the risk of your luggage being lost or delayed. Did you know each additional 10 pounds of luggage per traveler requires more than 300 million gallons of jet fuel per year? That's why there are now surcharges for luggage.

• Pack lightly if traveling by car, too, because an extra 100 pounds in the trunk equates to reducing your miles per gallon by up to 2 percent.

Dedicated to a green lifestyle

• Use the luggage tag that came with your suitcase instead of filling out a paper one at the ticket counter each time you fly. You'll save time, and the time of those behind you, not to mention paper.

PROBLEM: We run the risk of hurting those beautiful places we're going to enjoy.

Shades of Green

I can do that!

• Try eco-tourism. Plan a trip that focuses on environmental awareness. There are many Web sites that describe sustainable tourism, list eco-friendly destinations and offer extensive directories. Eco-tourism now accounts for about 20 percent of leisure travel.

• Travel during the off-season. This usually saves you money and you'll create less impact on the place you're visiting as you avoid crowds, lines and congestion.

• Familiarize yourself with and follow all local rules and regulations when visiting protected areas and wildlife habitats. Stay on the trails and leave places cleaner than you found them. Also maintain a safe distance from any animals you encounter.

• Take nothing but photographs and leave nothing but footprints.

• Light campfires only in established campfire rings and be sure all fires are completely extinguished before you leave the area.

• If you snorkel, do not touch the coral or stir up sediment. This can damage a reef's fragile ecosystem.

Takin' it to the next level

• Plan an adventure trip—hike, kayak or bike. It forces you to become actively engaged with new cultures, but might just make you more aware and respectful of the outdoors.

• Guide books are very helpful, but they don't know

everything. Venture out, talk to local people and venture off the beaten path.

• Buy souvenirs from local vendors and manufacturers rather than trinkets made somewhere else. It helps support the community you're visiting.

• Be thoughtful about what you buy. Don't buy souvenirs made from old-growth trees or derived from endangered forests or items made from endangered species. Chances are, you won't be able to get these items through U.S. Customs anyway.

• Eat in locally owned and operated restaurants. Try to find places that serve locally grown or produced food items.

Dedicated to a green lifestyle

• Bartering is expected –even anticipated—on trips to some destinations. While it's fun to get a bargain and be able to tell people how much you "saved," keep in mind that oftentimes you are a lot more well-off than your vendors. So, once again, support the local economy.

• If you're using a tour guide, choose one who exhibits a respect for the environment and encourages tourists to do the same.

• Consider a volunteer vacation. It's a great way to travel and do good at the same time.

PROBLEM: Poor choices in transportation can have the biggest negative environmental impact.

Shades of Green

I can do that!

• Taking a long road trip? If your personal vehicle is large or not very fuel-efficient, rent an economy car for your trip.
• The greenest and most affordable vacations are generally those that avoid planes and minimize driving. See what you can plan!

• Travel in groups. Be agreeable to sharing a taxi or using mass transit to save fuel.

• Cycle or walk during your trip. It's a great way to see local communities and meet local people firsthand. Plus, using your own muscle has great health benefits. And you're not adding carbon dioxide into the atmosphere.

Takin' it to the next level

• Seek out a hybrid taxi.

• If you rent a car, choose the smallest car that can comfortably accommodate you. And decline any "free upgrades" as they usually add to your cost of gas.

• If you rent a car make sure the car is well tuned and the tires are properly inflated. This will increase your gas mileage.

Dedicated to a green lifestyle

• Try an eco-friendly sailing cruise rather than a vacation aboard a cruise ship. Fewer passengers and less disruptions to ports are two great eco-friendly reasons.

Shades of Green

Cruise ships can spill oil and sewage and disrupt area wildlife. Did you know that a single cruise ship consumes several thousand gallons of fuel PER HOUR! Wind in your sails is free.

• Take into account the amount of carbon dioxide emitted from your flights. Then invest in "carbon offsets" or plant trees to offset that amount.

PROBLEM: We waste energy and other things at home while we're away.

I can do that!

• Put your lights on timers instead of leaving them on the entire time. The average household spends more than $12 a year on electricity to power a 100-watt bulb. Imagine the savings of a timer set for 8-12 hours versus a light on 24/7.

• Be sure to unplug appliances, where possible, before you go.

• Stop your mail. This saves post office fuel costs as well as the cost of having someone come over to take care of your mail and newspapers.

• Stop your newspaper. This stops waste and saves money. Most newspapers will credit your account for the days you're away or donate your newspapers to a school or senior citizen center.

• Turn your thermostat to 50 degrees F in cold months and 85 degrees F in warm months.

• Close your shades.

Shades of Green

Takin' it to the next level

• Turn down your water heater to its lowest setting. Did you know the U.S. uses $1 million worth of energy every minute? Help by turning down the dial.

• Eliminate all stand-by power.

Dedicated to a green lifestyle

• Turn your home's water off at its outside connection. This saves water and protects your home from flooding should a pipe break while you're gone.

• If you have a waterbed, turn down the waterbed heater at least 10 degrees.

Green Links and References

In this section we have provided you just a few of the hundreds (literally!) of websites that help people become more green and environmentally friendly in their lifestyles. They are listed in alphabetical order for ease of use.

This is by no means a comprehensive list, but a starting point to learn more. Do your own surfing after visiting these sites and you'll discover a whole "green world" available on the Internet.

AARP's Design for Living
www.aarp.org/families/home_design/universaldesign/design_for_living.html

Building Green
www.buildinggreen.com

Campaign Earth
www.campaignearth.org

Climate Counts
www.climatecounts.org

Conservation International: Living Green
www.conservation.org/act/live_green/

Shades of Green

Earth 911
www.earth911.org

Eartheasy: Sustainable Living
www.eartheasy.com

Energy Star
www.energystar.gov

Environmental Defense
www.environmentaldefense.org

Environmental Protection Agency
www.epa.gov

Friends of the Earth
www.foe.org

Green Footsteps
www.greenfootsteps.com

The Green Guide
www.thegreenguide.com

Green Hotels Association
www.greenhotels.com

Greenmill Village
www.greenmillvillage.com

Green Living ideas
www.greenlivingideas.com

GreenPeace
www.greenpeace.org

Shades of Green

The Independent Traveler
www.independenttraveler.com

Living Green from Co-op America
www.coopamerica.org/programs/livinggreen/

Modern Traveler Magazine
www.moderntravelermagazine.com

New American Dream
www.newdream.org

Natural Resources Defense Council Green Living Toolkit
www.nrdc.org/greenliving/toolkit.asp

Seventh Generation: Living Green
www.seventhgeneration.com/living_green/

Sierra Club
www.sieraclub.org

Treehugger
www.treehugger.com

U.S. Green Building Council
www.usgbc.org

Shades of Green

The Authors

Julie A. Vincent, APR

Julie has more than 25 years of experience in corporate communications, media relations, crisis management, marketing and writing services. She is president and owner of Wordsmith Communications Group, Inc., a full-service marketing communications consulting firm, and a public relations consultant for Roche Diagnostics Diabetes Care.

Right out of college, Julie taught journalism, English, speech and creative writing on the secondary level and still holds a lifetime teaching license in the state of Indiana. She is currently an adjunct professor at IUPUI in the Journalism department.

A published author and a national award-winning corporate communicator, Julie has a B.S. in Journalism, English and Radio/Television/Film from Ball State University and a M.S. in Journalism and Secondary Education from Butler University. She also has her APR designation from the Public Relations Society of America and is a past president of both the Hoosier Chapter of PRSA and the Indianapolis Public Relations Society.

Julie, her husband Dave, and their son Gavin live in Indianapolis.

Shades of Green

The Authors

Robert E. Dittmer, APR

Bob has more than 30 years experience in public relations, marketing and higher education.

His current position as a faculty member in the Indiana University School of Journalism at IUPUI is the culmination more than 15 years as an adjunct faculty member with colleges and universities around the country, in both graduate and undergraduate programs. He teaches public relations courses, is responsible for managing the public relations sequence, is director of the graduate program in public relations, and serves as the marketing and retention officer for the school.

A published author, Bob has written *151 Quick Ideas to Manage Your Time* and co-authored *151 Quick Ideas for Delegating and Decision Making and 151 Quick Ideas to Improve Your People Skills*. All three are published by Career Press.

He has served as the Director of Media Relations for both an American government organization with responsibilities for all of Europe, as well as for NATO with responsibilities for public information management worldwide. Bob has more than 20 years experience in public relations and advertising agencies working on a wide variety of clients in both Business-to-Business and Business-to-Consumer arenas.

With a B.A. from John Carroll University and an M.A. in Communication from Marshall University, and Accreditation from the Public Relations Society of America (PRSA), he is also dedicated to his profession. He was the 1998 President of the Hoosier Chapter, PRSA. He also served as 1999 Chair of PRSA's national Association Section and as Chair of PRSA's East Central District in 2001 (five states). Bob was elected to membership in the Indianapolis Public Relations Society in 1998.

Bob and his wife Susan live in Indianapolis.

www.ingramcontent.com/pod-product-compliance
Lightning Source LLC
Chambersburg PA
CBHW020257290526
45784CB00003B/1283